Praise for *The Luckiest*

"Kelly Cervantes is a truth-teller, full stop. I've seen the truth of her life and watched her fight for joy in the middle of heartbreak. She doesn't flinch from grief—instead, she invites her reader into the messy, beautiful reality of becoming. Rebuilding identity, love, and purpose when life doesn't go as planned. *The Luckiest* is a raw, grounded, and deeply human book. In these pages, Kelly isn't just offering a story—she's offering a hand in solidarity. Take it."

—Mary Katherine Backstrom, national bestselling
author of *Holy Hot Mess* and *Crazy Joy*

"It's rare to find a companion who is raw, real, vulnerable, nonjudgmental, inspiring, and truthful all at once. In Kelly's *The Luckiest*, I found this companion. As a mother, daughter, partner, sister, and person trying to navigate what it means to live a full life amidst heartbreak, I turned to *The Luckiest* for wisdom and reassurance, and I'm so much better for it. *The Luckiest* is for any of us who need to feel seen in our own strengths and insecurities."

—Myra Sack, award-winning author of *Fifty-Seven
Fridays: Losing our Daughter, Finding our Way*

"*The Luckiest* is a beautifully layered memoir that captures what it means to live through love, loss, and reinvention. With unflinching honesty and deep emotional intelligence, Kelly Cervantes reminds us that our scars—visible and invisible—can shape a life of meaning, resilience, and grace. Her story is a powerful reflection on the tenderness and tenacity it takes to keep going, even when the path forward is uncertain."

—Dr. Shoshana Ungerleider, internal medicine
physician and founder of End Well

"This stunning memoir lays bare the raw truth of becoming a mother, losing a child, and coming to terms with the fact that control is an illusion. It's a fearless, deeply human story about the power of hope, how grief reshapes us, and what it takes to find ourselves over and over again."

—Jessica Fein, author of *Breathtaking*

"Once again Cervantes offers the reader the gift of insight that comes only through holding great pain—that joy and hope are always tucked next to the names of your beloveds on the acknowledgement page of every album, book, and program of your life. Though we know that heartbreak of various kinds is inevitable in a full life, Kelly reminds us that it's worth it to do it all anyway."

—Meghan Riordan Jarvis, LICSW, author of *Can Anyone
Tell Me: Essential Questions About Grief and Loss*

"*The Luckiest* is heartfelt, brilliant, and revelatory. Kelly's writing has this rare, extraordinary quality of making you feel completely seen while simultaneously offering a glimpse into a world drastically different from your own. I found myself crying from how deeply I was moved, only to burst out laughing in the next breath. Her comedic timing is flawless and her insights hit home. Kelly's story will leave you with a renewed appreciation for life and for the people who make it so meaningful."

—Amy Shoenthal, bestselling author of *The Setback Cycle*

The
Luckiest

Also by Kelly Cervantes

Normal Broken

The
Luckiest

A Memoir of Love,
Loss, Motherhood, and the
Pursuit of Self

Kelly Cervantes

BenBella

BenBella Books, Inc.
Dallas, TX

BenBella

BenBella Books, Inc.
8080 N. Central Expressway, Suite 1700
Dallas, TX 75206
www.benbellabooks.com
Send feedback to feedback@benbellabooks.com

BenBella is a federally registered trademark.

Printed in the United States of America
10 9 8 7 6 5 4 3 2 1

Library of Congress Cataloging-in-Publication Data: 2025020239
ISBN 9781637747599 (hardcover)
ISBN 9781637747605 (electronic)

Editing by Victoria Carmody
Copyediting by Leah Baxter
Proofreading by Cheryl Beacham and Denise Pangia
Text design and composition by PerfecType, Nashville, TN
Cover design by Morgan Carr
Cover photo by Evie S. on Unsplash
Printed by Lake Book Manufacturing

Special discounts for bulk sales are available. Please contact bulkorders@benbellabooks.com.

*For the cherished companions whom we are
lucky enough to have hold our hands.*

*And for all my hand-holders,
but especially Mom, Dad, and Miguel.*

CONTENTS

How I picture it: We are all nesting dolls, carrying the earlier iterations of ourselves inside. We carry the past inside us. We take ourselves—all of our selves—wherever we go.

—Maggie Smith, *You Could Make This Place Beautiful*

INTRODUCTION

My favorite day of the year isn't my birthday, Christmas, or any other holiday for that matter. I can't even predict when it will occur. Typically, it's a day in March or April, one of the first days when I can step outside in a T-shirt or just a light jacket. The sun is shining, and my light-deprived skin hungrily absorbs the vitamin D.

Growing up in the Midwest and spending most of my adult years in the Northeast, I know pleasant weather at this time of year is not yet permanent. A late April snowstorm is always possible—a tulip's survival is as much a credit to the gardener's skill as the weather's temperament. But that only makes this first sign of spring, this whisper of summer, that much more precious. To indulge in such a day is a privilege I don't take lightly; my fortune at being able to do so only adds to the day's wonder.

I began celebrating days like this during my college years in Boston, bucking my rule-following ways to play hooky from class and walk the Freedom Trail or sneak into a game at Fenway Park. As my responsibilities have evolved, so have the ways I observe this day. Years have gone by where I've barely noticed it at all.

"Have you been outside yet today? It's beautiful," my husband says, leaning against the door of my office.

I look outside at our sun-soaked New Jersey driveway, the first of the perennial wild pansies sprouting at its edges.

1

This will not be one of those years.

"Anessa, want to go on an adventure to the park?" I ask my four-year-old daughter.

We find a path to explore. The creek we walk by is full from the recent rain and lined with trees that are beginning to flower, pink buds dotting their branches. We tiptoe past turtles, necks outstretched toward the sun, and watch red-breasted robins feast on bug buffets amidst the tall grasses.

Anessa skips and twirls several feet ahead of me until she comes across a playground in a clearing.

"Mommy! I've never been to this playground before!" She drags me across the wood chip–strewn ground, as excited as though we'd stumbled upon a secret garden or magical kingdom.

The various play structures are crawling with children of all ages, from those just learning to walk to middle schoolers avoiding home and the studies that await them. Most of the adults present are seated on the weathered wooden benches surrounding the playground. Those with younger, less-coordinated children are shadowing more closely behind them as they learn to climb, spin, and slide—ready to catch them should they fall.

Within minutes Anessa has found a new best friend and is two courses into a tea party. I take a seat on an empty bench within sight of Anessa and work hard to stay in the present. The day is too beautiful, this future memory too sweet, to allow the ghosts and what-ifs of my past to take over my mind.

Anessa may never have been to this playground before, but I have. It's been nine years and a lifetime since I watched my now-eleven-year-old son toddle through these wood chips. How naively hopeful I had been for a future that was never guaranteed. I close my eyes and ground myself in other sensations: the hard uneven earth beneath my feet, the slight breeze on my skin, children shouting, swings creaking. Suddenly self-aware, I open my eyes and scan the other mothers and caregivers, wondering what they see in me while reflexively assessing them.

Perhaps it's my introspective state, but in each of them I find a bit of myself:

In the hovering mother, forever wanting to keep her child in a protective bubble.

In the working mother taking these minutes to respond to just a few more emails. Eternally locked in the Sisyphean struggle toward work–life balance.

In the lonely mother anxiously making eye contact with any adult who will hold her gaze.

Their role as mother is most visible in this setting, but I know they are more than their relationship to others. I try to imagine what I don't see, what I can't see. The people they once were, their prior selves nestled at various depths below the surface:

The freshly independent adolescent navigating the adult world with the grace of a stumbling toddler.

The increasingly confident young professional negotiating the corporate world just as she once steered her way through the social hierarchy of her high school's hallways.

The grown woman struggling to let go of the false narratives she had absorbed as truth.

The grieving woman, forever reconciling her befores and afters, her luck and misfortune.

I wonder: Are we lucky if we escape life with soft skin and minimal layers? Or are we lucky to have the battle scars that show a life of survival and meaning?

I don't actually know any of these women's stories, and they don't know mine. My perceptions are a self-reflection of my own past identities, experiences, and relationships. Once upon a time, while sitting on one of these very park benches, I had planned for a life very different from the one I now lead. For years, I felt that life had been stolen from me, but it was never mine to begin with. Control over anything beyond what we can emotionally or physically manipulate in the current moment is perhaps life's grandest illusion of all.

A breeze rustles the tree leaves, bringing with it a familiar chill. I'm surprised to see how low the sun now hangs in the sky. Both are reminders of how fleeting and precious my favorite day can be.

"Anessa, it's time to go, sweetie."

Anessa resists, running from me, fully in the present without thought or concern for what is to come or what has come before.

I begin to walk away from the playground, a signal to my willful preschooler that I am serious about leaving.

"Mommy!" she yells from behind me.

I turn and smile, waiting for her to run up to me. She slips her hand into mine, and I give it a reassuring squeeze. As we head back past the birds, the budding trees, and the turtle-lined creek, I remind myself how, too often, I fail to appreciate the beauty around me.

But not today, this almost-warm, favorite, lucky day.

CHAPTER ONE
The Special Daughter

needed the red crayon—not orange-red, not red-orange, just plain red. The crayons were scattered on the beige carpeting in front of me, but I couldn't see it anywhere. Alice, our fifty-pound basset hound, had settled next to me. With all my eight-year-old strength, I tried pushing her out of the way to see if she was lying on top of it. Then I spotted it, the not-orange-red, not-red-orange, just-plain-red crayon. It had rolled under the couch, not under Alice—what luck! And thank goodness, because Alice wasn't budging, and no other color would do for She-Ra's cape. Laying on my belly, I outlined the Princess of Power's costume in my coloring book before filling it in, being careful not to color outside the lines.

"Daddy's home!" Mom announced from the kitchen, where she was making dinner.

"Daddy!" I yelled, greeting him from my place on the living room floor as he came up the stairs of our split-level house.

"Hey, Princess," Dad said, leaning down to give me a kiss on the top of my head. "Nice coloring. Where's your brother?" He freed his neck from the tie he wore to work each day and headed to the kitchen.

Dad worked at Union Pacific Railroad, which was headquartered in Omaha, Nebraska, where we lived. He did something in marketing or sales, but I wasn't sure what exactly.

"Hi there," Mom smiled.

She looked perfectly put together as always. Her Mary Kay makeup was precisely applied, just like the pictures in the tutorial pamphlets she took with her to the sales parties she hosted. She had worked as a nurse until I was three. Now, I was pretty sure she just worked because she liked to have her own money.

I dreamed of Mom driving us around in the pink Mary Kay Cadillac that the very highest-achieving salespeople were awarded. When I'd asked her when she would get her pink car, she'd said, "Oh honey, you have to sell a *lot* of makeup for that to happen, and then I wouldn't be able to spend as much time with you. But when you grow up you can work toward getting any kind of car you like. You can be whoever you want to be and do whatever you want to do." And I had believed her. Between Mom telling me I could achieve anything I set my mind to and Mister Rogers reminding me every beautiful day from his puppet-filled neighborhood that I was special, I accepted as fact that the only thing between me and greatness was personal effort.

Mom greeted Dad with a kiss before answering his question. "Cammie was playing outside with the neighbors, and then he fell asleep under the swing set," she said. Cameron had stopped taking scheduled naps before turning two earlier that year. But every once in a while, a nap would sneak up on him, and he would fall asleep wherever he had been playing. "Kelly, can you please go wake up your brother, and tell him dinner is almost ready? Then you can get your and Cammie's drinks for dinner."

Back turned to avoid being seen, I rolled my eyes in response, but dutifully rose from the floor to awaken Sleeping Beauty in the backyard.

I had been so excited to have a younger brother. However, due to Cameron's C-section birth, when I first saw my mother she was in the hospital bed with an oxygen cannula in her nose and an IV in her arm. Just like the people in the soap operas Mom and I used to watch together, right before they died and became ghosts haunting their ex-lovers. I'd burrowed my face in her armpit—all I could reach from beside the raised bed. I tried to be the strong big sister my family told me I would need to be, but I cried anyway.

Such a dramatic entrance for an ordinary little brother.

I opened the back door and hung onto the doorframe, swinging half my body outside. Just like Mom had said, Cam was sprawled in the grass like a giant starfish under our metal swing set, his Batman T-shirt hiked up to expose his toddler belly.

"Caaamerooon!" I yelled from the back door. Cam began to stir. "Wake up! It's dinner time!"

"Hey there, sleepyhead! What would you like to drink with dinner?" Mom asked Cam as he barreled inside, knocking over Alice's food bowl and scattering dog food all over the kitchen floor.

"I'm not Sleepyhead, I'm Batman!" he announced with his hands on his hips.

"Milk or water?" I asked. Cameron stared straight ahead as if he hadn't heard me. "Milk or water . . . Batman." I rolled my eyes again, this time not caring who saw me.

"Milk, please!" Cameron answered.

After dinner, Dad did the dishes and was responsible for making sure Cam and I bathed. Then he would turn on whatever baseball game was playing on basic cable and sit with me in front of our big box television with a spray bottle of Johnson & Johnson hair detangler while Mom put Cam to bed.

"*And that 6–4–3 double play will end the inning,*" the announcer said. The screen transitioned to a commercial.

"A double play is two outs," I recited.

"That's right, when a team gets two outs in a single play," Dad confirmed, lightly tugging the brush through my hair.

I genuinely enjoyed watching baseball, but I also knew that Dad would always engage with me if I was asking about America's, and his, favorite pastime. "But what do the numbers mean? 6-4-3?"

"All the defensive positions have a number. The pitcher is one, the catcher is two . . ."

While my father prioritized his relaxation, I don't remember my mother ever sitting still for enjoyment. Maybe to read a book—maybe—and then only if her to-do list was completed. From her well-kept home to her ever-patient demeanor, from her meticulous handwriting to her not-a-hair-out-of-place appearance, my mother aimed for, and usually achieved, perfection. As far as I was concerned, there was Mom's way and there was the wrong way.

Soon enough, Mom returned to the living room, Cameron now in bed. She immediately set about straightening the space, returning throw pillows to the couch and straightening blankets. "There is so much to get done before we leave on vacation next week," she said.

"You call that a strike, ump?!" Dad yelled at the TV. It's unclear whether he hadn't heard Mom or was trying to avoid the to-do list he was surely about to be handed.

That summer, instead of our usual trip to Lake Michigan with my Mimi and Grandad, we were going to drive all the way to Portland, Maine, visiting family and friends along the way. However, I was the most excited for our day trip to New York City. Mom had told me about a giant whale hanging from the ceiling of the Museum of Natural History (I hoped it was a humpback, my favorite!), and we were going to climb all the way up to the Statue of Liberty's crown.

With the living room straightened and my hair detangled, Mom turned to me: the next item on her to-do list.

"Okay, sweetie, it's your turn for bed," she said, coming to usher me down the hall to the bathroom to brush my teeth. I nodded in agreement and kissed Dad good night, his dark mustache scratching my skin.

Tucked in my lavender sheets, I imagined our day in New York City—or as Mom, who had been born and raised in New Jersey, called it, *the* city. As excited as I was for the museum and the Statue of Liberty, perhaps the best part was that Cameron was being left behind in Philadelphia with cousins, and it was going to be a special day with just Mom, Dad, and me. Don't get me wrong, I loved Cameron (still do!). But sharing the spotlight after six years of being an only child had been more jarring than I'd anticipated, and I was looking forward to a temporary return to the good ol' days.

That said, I did enjoy having Cameron around to play house and school, and to dress up as the groom for the pretend weddings I planned with our neighbors. He usually did what I asked him to, which was more than I could say for my friends at school. I didn't ask for much, really, just that people did what I wanted them to, when I wanted them to do it. My friends said that made me bossy, but how could you be the boss without being a little bossy?

In New York everyone was bossy, or at least that's what it seemed like in the movies. No one told Peter Venkman what to do in *Ghostbusters*, and when they tried, the city was taken over by ghosts! (I'd made Dad promise we would not be going anywhere near the New York Public Library since the ghost librarian from the opening scene still gave me nightmares. I knew it was just a movie, but I wasn't taking any chances.)

But even with specters out of the picture, I just knew visiting New York was going to be an exciting day, full of bossy people doing special things. And I couldn't wait to join them.

CHAPTER TWO
The Different One

I have a hard time differentiating between my personal memories from our trip to New York City and the secondhand memories I've pieced together from photographs and stories. Mostly, I remember being upset that it was a blue whale, not a humpback whale, hanging from the ceiling of the Museum of Natural History. But I also remember how different the people were that roamed the museum, climbed the narrow steps inside the Statue of Liberty, and strolled by our taxicab window. There wasn't just every shade of skin, but also varied clothing styles, cultural influences, and languages. No two groups walked, talked, or held themselves the same way. Compared to Omaha, where my community was safe albeit sheltered, pleasant though homogenized, and where I had perceived sameness as valued, this unapologetic difference seemed rebellious and thrilling. It turns out it wasn't just their bossiness that made New Yorkers special; it was also their differences.

Had we visited New York two years earlier, when I was six, I doubt that I would have had the same reaction to the city's bustle and diversity. But by the time I was eight, I was already two years into the theater classes my first-grade teacher had recommended to my mother to help ease my shyness. In theater class, differences weren't shunned but explored: our voices were encouraged, our imaginations were cultivated, and we were taught the value of coloring outside the lines. Classes turned into camp, which by middle school became auditioning for the community theater's mainstage shows. I loved every aspect of performing, from the thrill of stepping out under the lights to the audience's approving applause.

With every community theater production, there were a few weekday matinee performances scheduled for student field trips. These were the most exciting because I got to miss my morning classes, returning just in time for lunch. Typically, I performed in shows with a dozen other children, but in seventh grade I was cast as "The Doll" in *Inspector Gadget*. It was a forgettable part with only one or two lines, but I got to wear a padded suit and bright blue eyeshadow, and I was the only kid in the production. This was peak special.

After one matinee performance, to miss as little school as possible, I took my stage makeup off in the car instead of in my dressing room (I had a dressing room! It was shared, but still). With the visor mirror open, I began carefully removing the apple red from my cheeks and mouth, leaving the eyeshadow.

"You sure you don't want to take it all off?" Mom asked.

"No, I like how it looks," I said confidently. To be clear, I was wearing clown makeup.

After proudly presenting my note at the front office explaining my tardiness was due to a theater performance, I headed to the cafeteria to meet up with friends in the lunch line. It didn't take long for the snickering to begin.

"Look at her . . . behind us . . ." a popular girl said, rolling her eyes.

"What is on her face?" her friend asked, laughing.

I shrank in the line, trying to hide, but more people were beginning to stare.

Cassie, one of my more assertive friends, said loudly enough for the entire line to hear, "It is so cool that you get to miss school to act on stage," and I managed a weak smile of thanks.

As soon as I'd dropped my tray at our lunch table, I excused myself to the bathroom. When I was sure I was alone, I wetted the commercial-grade paper towel and began removing all evidence of my public shaming. The rough paper transformed my eyelids from a vibrant blue to a raw red. How could I have been so stupid? What was wrong with me?

Omaha was not New York.

WHILE I DESPERATELY wanted to be liked, I struggled to assimilate. I could dress the part, copying the trends worn by the popular girls, but there was this part of me tucked deep where I couldn't squash it that needed to be different. It wasn't just that I felt different and didn't fit in (find me a middle schooler that doesn't feel that way). I *needed* to be different, to stand out, to live up to the specialness my mom and Mister Rogers saw within me.

Throughout middle school, I tried on different friend groups like a toddler playing dress-up. It wasn't until my freshman year of high school that I found the theater kids. My middle school hadn't put on theatrical productions, but the high school did three shows a year and had a competitive speech and acting team. In the cast and crew and my teammates, I found friends who also yearned to feel special, and in our director and coach, Mr. Peterson, I found a second father figure who encouraged ambition and never asked or expected us to be anyone but ourselves.

The safe space Mr. Peterson provided was significant given how conservative and insular our corner of Omaha was at the time. As with many other Midwest cities and towns, a history of racial segregation meant that Omaha lacked neighborhood diversity, with communities coalescing along racial and ethnic lines. Aside from the occasional tournament or athletic event, my classmates and I rarely left our homogenous vanilla enclave.

At my already mostly white high school, everyone was expected to have certain other things in common as well. Every Tuesday morning, I either had to join in with or walk around the hundred or so kids that prayed around the flagpole. They weren't praying in memoriam or anything; it was just a thing some students organized. On Wednesdays, there were no extracurricular activities scheduled after school because everyone attended their church's youth group that day—myself included. Some of my friends even received promise rings from their significant others or fathers, the promise being to wait until marriage to have sex. I know there must have been kids who were doing things like drinking, smoking, and having sex, but I wasn't friends with them. I never even attended a party in high school where there was alcohol.

Though, as I would learn, that didn't mean attending parties came without social risk. "Kelly, truth or dare?" Lauren asked me, sitting up on her sleeping bag. It was sophomore year, and me and five of my girlfriends from school were circled up in our pj's in Lauren's basement. Our sleeping bags were fanned out behind us, the carpet before us littered with chip bags, nail polish, and teen magazines.

"Truth," I answered. Typically, the safer choice.

"Will you have sex before you're married?"

Ashley looked up from painting her toenails. Megan stopped eating mid-chip.

Should have gone with dare . . .

I knew Mom had had sex before marriage because I'd asked her, and as I've already established, Mom is basically perfect. Still, I hesitated. "Um, I don't know, probably?" I answered, as noncommittal as possible.

My friends fell silent and exchanged looks for a few seconds. Then the shaming began.

"Don't you want to stay pure for your husband?"

"What if he won't marry you because you're not a virgin?"

"You can only go to heaven if you wait until you're married."

I was mortified.

The irony of it all was that it was actually my church friends who were my "bad" friends. It was on a church mission trip that one of my friends came out to me. Another friend on the trip explained the basics of giving a blowjob—and thank goodness for that, because I was genuinely surprised to learn there was more sucking than blowing involved.

I was pretty sure being slut-shamed for even *thinking* about sex before marriage was a little over the top. I had snuck episodes of *Beverly Hills, 90210*, and those kids were doing so much worse. Mom said the show was inappropriate, though she had made an exception for the episode where Brenda has a breast cancer scare because I convinced her that one was educational (RIP Shannen Doherty). But even if *90210* was also an extreme, I figured the truth had to lie somewhere in the middle . . . right?

Despite the threat of scarlet letter pariahdom, I rebelled privately. My journals were filled with lists of the boys I had crushes on and what they had done that week to move them up or down the list. I played out scenes with my reflection in the bathroom mirror, fantasizing about how I would respond if one of those boys ever asked me out. But while my friends were imagining how many children they wanted to have, I was imagining the acting awards I would surely one day receive. Omaha may have been home, but even at fifteen I needed that to be just for now, not forever.

In the meantime, just to be safe, I kept my dreams in my journals and made sure everyone else saw me continuing to color inside the lines.

BY SENIOR YEAR, most of my more conservative friends had graduated. In their absence, I found myself leaning into new friendships, specifically with Courtney and Brittany. (Could you find three girls with more '80s names?) While we had been friendly since middle school, up to that point we hadn't spent a lot of time outside of school together. Now, between attending Friday night football games (a social must) and play practices, we began recording ridiculous skits with Brittany's camcorder in my bedroom.

With Courtney and Brittany, I didn't feel like I needed to keep my guard up in the same way I had with my other friends. We weren't totally certain what we wanted to do with our lives, but we agreed that we wanted a career before starting a family. Instead of discussing our future children's names, we talked about the countries we wanted to visit, the cities we might live in, the different kinds of people we would meet. None of us quite felt like we fit in in Omaha: Brittany had the worst case of wanderlust I have ever known, my ambition had long outgrown the confines of The Cornhusker State, and Courtney, well, she was Jewish.

"I got another note in my locker," Courtney told me as we passed each other in the hallway between classes. "I think I'm going to talk to the principal about it."

For months, Courtney and several other Jewish students had been finding notes in their lockers inviting them to a church youth group. In case the message wasn't clear enough, several students had also told Courtney to her face that she was going to hell if she didn't convert. The principal, who may or may not have agreed with the perpetrators, said there was nothing the school could do about it. Suddenly, the safe and pleasant, albeit sheltered and homogenized community I'd grown up in felt considerably less safe or pleasant.

Courtney was kind and thoughtful. She acted more like Jesus taught than many of the Christians I knew. But because she was born into a Jewish family, she was going to hell unless she disowned the people she loved and abandoned their millennia of beliefs and traditions?

Unable to reconcile the good in my friend with the scripture our classmates used to justify their condemnations, I turned to my parents and pastor.

"You can boil the Bible down to one rule: treat others the way you wish to be treated," Mom said. "The rest is just examples of how and why."

My pastor counseled that it was up to God, not individuals, who was saved and that God took deeds rather than just religious belief into consideration. These conversations helped console me—at least *my* religion didn't think my best friend was going to hell—but now that I had started asking questions, I couldn't stop.

How much of my lot in life—for example, the fact I didn't face daily discrimination—was because I was born into the "right" kind of family, something that was entirely out of my control? Was that just luck? And why should something as uncontrollable as luck have any say in how people were treated, anyway?

I realized that maybe wanting to be special wasn't such a rare thing after all—except instead of trying to earn specialness through good works and achievement, some people were trying to feel special by pushing others down. Maybe I had it wrong: instead of sameness being valued, difference was feared. And if that was the case, what was I really risking if I chose to color outside of the lines?

Without clear answers, and unable (unwilling?) to turn off the torrent of questions flooding my mind, I instead committed to controlling every aspect of my life that didn't already rest in luck's clenched fist. Starting with my future.

CHAPTER THREE
The Codependent

Choosing control over luck meant even though I had stood in front of my mirror countless times practicing my Oscar acceptance speech, I would not be pursuing an acting degree. The limitless variables that determined whether an artist was starving or successful terrified me. Well, that and Dad didn't want to pay for a BFA. I didn't know what else I wanted to do, though. I still kept up with professional sports, so maybe something in Major League Baseball? Or on the business side of the entertainment industry? Who knew?! Not me!

All I knew was my very next step: after graduation, I was off to Northeastern University in Boston. I couldn't wait to experience life beyond suburbia. Boston felt just big enough to be exciting but not overwhelming. Like New York City with training wheels. Courtney was also headed east for college, bound for a university thirty minutes outside of Boston. So I wouldn't be completely alone out there. Instead of being terrified by the blank slate before me, I saw endless opportunity. Eventually, something would pique my interest or someone would see something in me, my path would unfold, and wherever it led I would overachieve every step of the way.

Everything was going according to plan. Right up until the month before I left for Boston, which would be a rapid-fire initiation into young adulthood. Amidst the excitement of getting my first cell phone, I also had my first introductions to debilitating anxiety and disordered eating. It began when my boyfriend of three months broke up with me. Sitting on my bed sobbing into my mom's arms, I actually uttered the words "but he told me he loved me!" Heartbreak, I would learn, isn't soothed by clichés.

That grief would pale in comparison, though, to the passing of a dear friend's mother from cancer. This wasn't my first exposure to death—my Mimi had passed away when I was ten—but teenagers weren't supposed to lose their parents. This new reality disrupted everything I thought I understood about the way the world worked. And as is too often the case, it took witnessing this loss for me to realize how precious my own family was to me . . . and that I was about to go 1,500 miles away to a school where I couldn't come home on the weekends if I got homesick.

It started as nausea whenever I tried to eat. At first, I truly believed that there was something wrong with my stomach. Mom took me to a gastrointestinal doctor, but after I choked down a barium drink and got some X-rays, my results came back clear. A few weeks later, my physical symptoms were lessening, but I quite liked the number on the scale and the new way I looked. This was the age of Britney Spears and Christina Aguilera, SlimFast and diet everything; there was no such thing as too skinny. By the time my pediatrician suggested that perhaps I was experiencing anxiety, I had already embraced the control I could exert over my body in the face of so much uncertainty.

The week before I was set to leave for college, Mom and Dad confronted me. "We've talked to your doctor," they told me, "and if you don't start eating and gaining weight, we are in agreement that we can't let you go to Boston."

Wouldn't you know it? I was miraculously cured.

So with my anxiety and eating disorder neatly tucked away in my luggage and my brand-new cell phone in my pocket, I boarded a plane to Boston.

WITH ITS MAZE of cobblestone streets (in which I would get countless stiletto heels stuck), Boston was a world away from Omaha. It was impossible to walk to class and not feel the impression of centuries of history. I was struck by how different New Englanders were from Midwesterners. How they favored bluntness and efficiency over politeness and niceties. How little they were concerned with religion and how much more they discussed their ethnic heritage—a detail I didn't know about even my closest high school friends, though I could easily recite the church or synagogue each one attended. Once, I even went on a date with a boy just because I was enthralled by his Boston accent. I'm sure I got homesick in the beginning, but I never wanted to leave.

I made friends in my classes and treated my longing for home by befriending and watching sports with the boys who lived in the dorm room above mine. Sports were my water wings. I could tread out into social situations because I had SportsCenter to fall back on.

Still, by winter break, I was excited to return home. My only hesitation was around seeing the boy from my high school whom I'd been exchanging messages with for the last few months.

Back in the spring, when I found out that my senior prom date had been making out with another girl (we weren't exclusive at the time, but I was still inexplicably enraged), I had accepted a new prom invitation from an incredibly unlikely source. Ryan was a popular athlete who never took an honors class and had zero extracurricular activities in common with me. We had been introduced by the one kid who both played football and did theater.

We had fun at prom together. Ryan was cute and incredibly goofy, but our wildly different social circles and the end of the school year prevented anything else from developing. But now we were both in college and growing into new identities away from the social constructs of high school . . . and we had been flirting online for months. Fun and harmless when I was a flight away—but now I was home again for break.

"Guess what?" Ryan asked me. We were sitting on my family's couch watching a movie with Cameron on one of the sleepy days between Christmas and New Year's.

"What?" I lifted my head from his shoulder to look at him.

"Chicken butt!" Ryan replied. Cameron burst out laughing. Ryan looked thoroughly pleased with himself.

I rolled my eyes and playfully punched his shoulder.

"Careful, Princess, I need that arm," he teased, before kissing my forehead and shifting me back into his arms.

God, he was cheesy. But he also felt safe.

He bent his head down to whisper in my ear. "You have no idea how beautiful you are," he said, quiet enough that Cameron couldn't hear.

Sure, he was cocky, but that only made the contrast of his adoration that much more meaningful. To Ryan I was special; he made me feel special. After ringing in the new year together, we decided to give a long-distance relationship a try. An interesting choice going into our second semesters of college. But instead of feeling constrained by the relationship, I found it liberating—initially, anyway.

"WANT TO SKIP class and go for a walk?" Declan's message dinged on my laptop screen. Outside, my neighbors were lounging in the sun-soaked courtyard, and a saxophone riff from a Dave Matthews Band song was blasting through an open window. In the distance, I could hear the crowd roar at Fenway Park—the Red Sox must have been playing an early season day game.

The weather had been getting warmer, the sun finally breaking through the grey of a long Boston winter. In the shade cast by Boston's taller buildings, there was probably still a chill, but in the sunshine, I would soon discover my favorite day of the year.

"Meet you outside your dorm in two minutes." I typed back. Omaha Kelly would never have cut class. But Boston Kelly was exploring boundaries and testing her free will. Especially now that she no longer felt the societally imposed threat of eternal damnation.

I had met Declan in one of my communication studies classes. He was from New England, a singer/songwriter, and proudly Irish. We bonded over our similar taste in music, from Ben Harper to David Gray. He taught me how to take a hit from a bong and then defended my innocence when his RA came to investigate the suspicious smell permeating the hallway. I could tell from the way I caught him looking at me that he would happily have been more than friends, but I was grateful he never pushed for more.

That afternoon we strolled aimlessly away from campus until we came across the Freedom Trail: a redbrick path cut into the sidewalk that winds its way through Boston's many historical sites. We let the weathered bricks guide our way as we chatted about roommate drama, summer plans, and concerts we wanted to attend.

It was an absolutely perfect day spent with a new friend.

By the time I made it back to my dorm room, Fenway Park was quiet, and The Dave Matthews Band had been traded out for Nelly. I also discovered that my cell phone had died. After plugging it in, I woke up my laptop from its laser-lined screensaver and was alarmed to find a flurry of messages from Ryan.

Hey Princess! . . . Hello? . . . Where are you? . . . Why aren't you answering your phone? . . . Are you ok? . . . Who are you with?

I'm so sorry! My phone died. It was our first warm day here. I ditched class and walked around Boston with a friend, I typed back.

What friend?

I spent the next few minutes promising Ryan that Declan and I were just friends, that nothing happened between us that day or ever, and that Ryan had nothing to worry about. He said he was being protective. Had I not still been a teenager, I might have questioned who he was protecting.

BACK HOME FOR the summer, Ryan and I were inseparable. Which was convenient—because as long as we were together, there was no need for Ryan to worry about me. If I ever felt concerned about his unwavering devotion, I didn't let it distract me from polishing the glittering pedestal he'd placed me on.

When I returned to college in the fall, I was determined to find a way to get Ryan to come east. Which was what led me to knock on the door of the athletic coach's office. Looking over the coach's shoulder in that windowless room, I directed him to pull up Ryan's stats.

"His school is NAIA, not NCAA, so he can transfer and play immediately without breaking any collegiate rules." I explained to the coach. "But he'll need a scholarship."

I had certainly grown more confident since starting college, but this was next-level ballsy, even for me. I didn't know the coach. I didn't even know anyone on the team. But I knew I loved Boston and had fallen for this boy—and that I needed to bring the two together.

So I did.

Ryan enrolled at Northeastern University to start the second semester of his sophomore year and was wearing a Husky uniform that spring.

In the early years of our relationship, Ryan provided me with all the verbal affirmation I yearned for, never letting me forget how beautiful I was and how he would always protect me. And at six foot three with washboard abs, he was easy to believe. But again, who or what was he protecting me from?

"I have a late practice, but I'll call you when I'm done." Ryan told me while walking me to my class one day. "Oh, and Mike's having a party tomorrow. I'll get the info tonight."

"Is it cool if I bring Kristin and Lindsay?" I had new roommates this year, and chances were that if I wasn't with Ryan, studying, or at a meeting for one of the clubs I belonged to, then I was with them.

"What if it's just us, and then you can get to know the other girl-friends better?" he asked. This wasn't the first time Ryan had pressured me to get closer with his teammates' girlfriends and spend less time with Kristin and Lindsay.

"Just ask," I said before standing on my tiptoes to kiss him goodbye. The confidence I derived from being with Ryan was intoxicating. It almost made me forget the control he was trying to exert over my life.

THE TYPICAL NORTHEASTERN undergrad attends college for five years, with the academic year evenly split between classes and "co-op," aka internships—the idea being that by graduation, not only do you have a degree, but you also have two years of work experience. This was a major reason I chose the school. I had imagined it would be the perfect opportunity to try out different career fields, since I had been desper-ately trying to find anything that interested me as much as performing.

By my middler (aka third) year of college, my continuing lack of career direction and clear vision for the future had become a personal paranoia. Where was the path I had been so certain would eventually appear before me? Further complicating my need for rational, if not traditional, plans was that I had enrolled in an elective acting class. And then I was looking up local talent agencies. And then I was going on photo shoots and trying to pull together a modeling portfolio. And then I was right back to dreaming of sitting across from David Letter-man telling him all about my new movie.

If Ryan didn't like me spending time with people he didn't know, he *really* didn't like the photo shoots. When it came to my social life, it was easier to let Ryan exert control than to argue with him—and besides, I genuinely liked hanging out with his teammates. But when it came to my classes, extracurricular activities, and hobbies, like acting or modeling, I adamantly did what I wanted. That didn't stop him from finding other ways to discourage me.

"You shouldn't squeeze your ass like that, it gets dimply," Ryan commented once as he entered my bedroom.

I had been lying across my bed naked, waiting for him. Face flushed, I quickly sat up and reached for the covers. Before then, I hadn't noticed my cellulite.

"You should start doing calf lifts in the shower. It will give your legs more definition," Ryan said one morning before leaving my apartment for class. Before that moment, I hadn't thought much about my muscle definition.

And so it went.

I don't remember Ryan critiquing my eating habits, but he didn't need to. Between his comments about my body and my insecurities surrounding my future, I was once again finding comfort in controlling my calorie intake. So what if I told myself that I would stop trying to lose weight when I reached 115 pounds—and then kept going? So what if I was so hungry that I binged junk food and sweets at a holiday party and then found an isolated bathroom on campus to puke in? It was a one-time thing, I told myself, a rectified mistake—while remaining vague as to whether the mistake had been the bingeing, the purging, or something else.

After I nearly passed out at the mall with Ryan, he threatened to call my mom and tell her I hadn't been eating. If my parents found out, I knew they would force me to come home immediately.

"Please don't tell my mom," I begged Ryan from a mall bench. "I promise I'll start eating more." As if to prove it, I took another bite of the pretzel he'd bought for me.

I kept my promise. The more I had tried to control my body, the more out of control my life had spiraled anyway. In place of food restriction, I allowed myself to become increasingly dependent on Ryan, not just for a social life but also for my self-worth.

Ryan had helped me to eat more again, so surely, I thought, that was a sign of how much he loved me, of how I could trust him. It would be years before I realized he had simply solved a problem he'd helped perpetuate. But at that moment, I loved him and he loved me and I loved being loved. Even still, I winced whenever he spoke about our future together. As I wrote in my journal, it felt at times like "Ryan and my heart were making plans without me."

Without my own clearly defined dreams, it was easier to lean into Ryan's. If I could support him in his athletic career, then perhaps that could be enough to fulfill me.

I didn't even need to say the words out loud to recognize their hollowness.

CHAPTER FOUR
The Pathfinder

While searching for my next co-op internship, I reached out to my family to see if they had any interesting leads. My cousin in Los Angeles responded and offered me the opportunity to stay at her home and work for her in the fitness industry. Ryan had committed to playing in an elite league out of town, so this seemed as good a time as any to explore LA and its age-old siren call.

So the summer after my twenty-first birthday, I moved in with my cousin's family, working out of her guesthouse during the day and host-essing in the evenings at Gladstones, a touristy restaurant overlooking the Pacific Ocean, to earn extra money.

From across the dining room, a server named Alex would catch my eye. Instead of looking away, he held my gaze. He was headed to Denmark soon to start a master's program in international relations, or something else intimidatingly smart. His tousled brown hair and ocean blue eyes didn't hurt, but it was his quiet confidence that drew me most. The way he'd reach low for my hand and give it a light squeeze as I passed him on my way back to the host stand. It was such a departure from the overt cockiness to which I'd grown accustomed.

You have a boyfriend, Kelly, I reminded myself over and over and over again.

Something about LA had me feeling unmoored, perhaps even a little erratic. No one knew me here, and even my cousin hadn't seen me since I was a little girl. Without Ryan hovering over me, my inner flame was hungrily feeding on fresh oxygen, and it was intoxicating. I didn't feel like myself, and there was no one around to remind me who I was—or to hold me accountable for any poor decisions I might make.

Within weeks of arriving, I stopped thinking about a life dictated by Ryan's athletic career and began dreaming again about a future of my own. What if I did pursue an acting career? Could I support myself with working at restaurants between whatever jobs I booked, like so many of my coworkers at Gladstones did? I felt like Dorothy walking out of her sepia-toned house and into technicolor Munchkinland. I had never felt more alive . . . or terrified.

My phone calls with Ryan did not do much to steady or ground me. "Where were you? Why didn't you pick up?" he asked, answering my call after one ring. It was late, and I was just getting home after grabbing a drink with coworkers. I looked longingly at my bed.

"Hello to you too." By now, I was used to these questions from Ryan, and more often than not I accepted them as our normal. "We were at a bar, and it was loud. I wouldn't have been able to hear you."

"Then you should have left the bar to talk to me. Who is more important to you?" He was slurring his words, which did not bode well for me going to sleep anytime soon.

"You are, Ryan. I love *you*. Just you, I promise."

"Then why didn't you leave? Who were you with?"

"Just some friends from work. You'll meet them when you come to visit." After another five to ten minutes of reassuring Ryan of my devotion and faithfulness, he finally let me go.

In the two and a half years Ryan and I had been together, I had never once even thought about another guy (*until Alex*). I was happy in our relationship (*wasn't I?*). And I was so lucky to be with Ryan. After all, what more could I want from a boyfriend (*besides maybe a little trust*)?

Though considering what happened next, I realize that was a touch hypocritical.

RYAN'S RINGTONE CARRIED above the din of the party all the way to the upstairs bathroom where I was currently pinned between Alex and a rose-pink wall, clearly tiled circa 1978.

I hadn't planned on ending up half naked in a bathroom making out with Alex. I mean, I'd fantasized about it, but I had a boyfriend— albeit a boyfriend who already accused me of cheating on him. Still, one exciting night would not be worth the resulting guilt, or so I had tried to convince myself.

But then Alex had sought me out at a house party, taking a seat next to me on an outdoor bench so small that it basically forced us to cuddle. I'd been chatting with other friends. But when Alex joined, my vision narrowed. He asked me about my family, my internship. He shared how excited he was for his master's program but admitted there were people in LA he was going to miss. *Does that include me? Would he miss me?*

Alex was thoughtful in his questions and honest in his responses. He shifted his arm so it was lightly touching my back.

I shivered, even though the heat of the day had yet to dissipate.

"You okay?" he asked, a knowing smile on his lips.

"Yeah . . ." I smiled, back leaning into him. *Never better.*

"Come here, I want to show you something." Alex had then taken my hand, leading me inside the house and up the stairs. I had knowingly and willingly followed.

At the sound of Ryan's ringtone, I threw on my shirt and rushed downstairs to find my phone before it sent him to voicemail. Not because I felt guilty, but because I didn't want to have to deal with the accusations, even if this time they were true. As I confessed to my journal the next day, "I had more fun yesterday before 3:45 AM than I have in so long." Did consequences even exist in LA? Especially if no one found out?

A few days later Alex was off to Denmark, and aside from a few emails, we never spoke again. Meanwhile, I continued to parry Ryan's accusations while desperately trying to allay my own misgivings. How could I have been so attracted to someone that wasn't Ryan? Why didn't I feel bad about what had happened? And was I really ready, at twenty-one, to be in the last relationship of my life?

But after I had been with Ryan for three and a half years, it wasn't just that I didn't know what *life* looked like without him: I didn't know who *I* was without him. Perhaps more concerning was that under these clear Californian skies, I didn't know who I was right now. When Courtney and then Kristin came to visit, I asked them to stay. When Ryan visited, I clung to him for dear life. By the time my parents came, I crumbled before them in tears.

At my parents' suggestion, I left LA early and came home for a bit before returning to Boston. Up to that point, I couldn't have imagined a scenario where I gave up an opportunity and accepted defeat at the hands of—what? My emotions? I knew I was unwell because I agreed.

However, even at home, surrounded by the love and support of my family, with all the reminders of who I was and what I valued, and with weekly visits to a psychiatrist (mandated by Mom), I struggled to reconcile my feelings for Ryan with how much more alive I'd felt away from him.

I returned to Boston more grounded but with lingering memories of a more independent life. As if waking from a dream, I registered how much I had already given up for Ryan. Aside from Kristin and Lindsay, my two incredibly patient roommates, I had few close friends. Ryan hadn't meshed well with the guys who'd lived above me freshman year, and so we'd grown distant. A friendship with Declan had been discouraged, and so it had faded like all the others.

Still, once I was reunited with Ryan, my doubts didn't last. I manically swung back and forth, craving more control but terrified of what life without him would look like—especially when my world had already grown so small. Then there was the simple fact that I loved him and he loved me. And how could anyone ever know me and love me the way he did? In order to protect the imperfect life I knew, I chose to sacrifice an independent future because there was nothing scarier than a life unplanned. We began talking about marriage, my parents gifted me my Mimi's wedding ring at Christmas, and the margins of my class notes filled with sketches of bridesmaid dresses.

When Ryan got drafted to play professionally, I thought that this was what it had all been for. The happy ending that would justify everything. And it might have if my life up to that point had been a movie, and we were now sitting in a dimly lit theater watching the credits roll.

Instead, our story continued, and when Ryan left for rookie camp a few weeks later, my flame once again devoured the open air, and my doubts returned—along with Ryan's unmitigated jealousy.

"You turned your phone off on purpose!" he yelled through the phone.

"I didn't—my phone died. Let's talk about it in the morning when you're thinking clearly," I said, talking him down for the umpteenth time, and hung up.

While catching up with my high school friend Brittany a few days later, she asked me if I thought I would be able to tell if Ryan were abusive.

"Yeah, I'd know the difference," I told her, but I wasn't sure.

WITH THE HELP of a few scattered trips to see him, Ryan and I lasted another tumultuous five months. Each visit scabbed over the biting words we'd flung at each other in between. But once his season was over and he was back in Boston for a longer visit, the extent of the damage was evident. We had both been pushing each other away, wanting to experience a life apart without actually wanting to be the one to end it.

The week after our visit, he finally made the call. "I'm not ready to settle down yet," he said. "I want one last dip in the sea before getting married."

I didn't try and change his mind.

I'd known that it would have to be Ryan that did it. It had to be his choice. At the time, I thought it was because I wasn't strong enough to do it. But the truth was that I thought we had a better chance of staying broken up if he was the one who decided to end it.

But just because I was relieved the relationship was over didn't make the breakup any less devastating.

"Did he actually say he needed 'one last dip in the sea'?" Kristin asked, pouring me wine as Lindsay served my favorite pasta.

I nodded through tears.

"Who says that? God, he's dumb," Lindsay snapped.

Best. Roommates. Ever.

AT TWENTY-TWO, I had grown up so much from the innocent eighteen-year-old who had fallen for the hometown boy. But I still wasn't sure who I was or who I wanted to be. I spent the rest of my senior year reconnecting with old friends and making up for the fact that I had been in a relationship the previous four. There was a lot of dancing, a few mistakes, and a whole lot of tears.

There is something so big and vulnerable about first love. It was unfathomable to me that I could ever love someone else that much. That anyone could ever understand me as well as Ryan had. More importantly, how could I ever try to love again if it meant giving someone else access to hurt me like that? There was no fucking way.

I harbored delusions of getting back together with Ryan *someday,* and we kept each other just close enough to allow the boundaries of our relationship to blur for a year or so. But finally, I found the courage, or the distance, to tell him to stop contacting me (*for real this time!*).

Now, decades later, all I can muster for my younger self—and Ryan's—is compassion. We were so young, one person's insecurities feeding off the other's like a serpent eating its own tail. Our time together shaped me into part of who I am today. But it did not make me.

When I left Omaha for Boston I thought I was breaking from the conservative culture I'd grown up in—that I was redrawing the lines I'd spent my childhood coloring inside of. But all I'd really done was transfer the ownership of those lines from the religious beliefs of others to Ryan. With ties cut and my future fully back in my hands, I was ready to draw my own lines in thick black permanent marker, and I was surprised to realize I already knew where I wanted those lines to lead.

Separating myself from Ryan had felt impossibly difficult. But drawing my own lines wasn't proving to be much easier. Specifically, telling my parents that I was going to move to New York to pursue an acting career after graduation.

"We're supposed to go after our dreams, right? Like how I want to play professional baseball," my brother Cameron offered, trying to support me.

"Yeah, we're not too worried about that happening," Dad shot back. Cam slumped in his dining chair. Mom rested a hand of support on his leg.

"At least she'll have her degree to fall back on," Mom reminded Dad.

I'd graduated with a degree in communication studies with a dual concentration in public speaking and organizational communication, with a double minor in business and religious studies. I'm not sure what that mouthful screams more: *Hi, I'm an overachieving eldest daughter,* or *I really wanted a theater degree but earned all these other ones instead.*

Weeks earlier I'd told Mom of my plan, but this was the first time Dad was hearing the news. My dad is not an angry man, but you don't have to look far to see where my dramatic tendencies come from. He is also hardwired to mitigate risk, to the point that his contingency planning can at times seem compulsive. Scrounging for auditions in the most populated US city was not checking those boxes for him. But I was twenty-three, and he couldn't stop me.

Dad and I didn't talk much over the next few months, mostly communicating through Mom instead. I certainly didn't tell him that I had hitched a ride to New York from Boston in the cab of the truck with my movers—who I only knew because Kristin had gone on a date with one of them.

Since getting upset about the blue whale at the Museum of Natural History as a child, I had only been back to New York a couple times: once on a quick weekend trip junior year of college with Ryan, and once to visit Courtney, who had moved to New York one year ahead of me. None of my previous visits could compare to seeing the city lights for the first time and knowing *this city* was my home. I'm sure I glowed with the same hope, promise, and naivety as all the other transplants who dreamed of making their name in New York.

Due to Ryan's isolating behavior, I had lost touch with many of my friends from high school, so after we broke up, I eagerly reconnected with them as well. Thanks to the recent advent of Facebook, this was remarkably easier than it would have been just a few years earlier. It turned out that my buddy Jeff was also planning on moving to New York, and after some back and forth about the timing, we decided to be roommates. Astoria, Queens, just outside of Manhattan, had been recommended to both of us as a great place to find relatively affordable housing.

Our first New York home was a converted one-bedroom apartment—meaning we turned the dining room into a bedroom by sectioning it off with a tension rod and a dollar store curtain. The central focus of the apartment was a brown and tan striped futon purchased from a discount furniture store down the street, and the final touch was a framed photo of Jeff and me at his junior prom when I was just a cherub-faced sophomore. It was one of those awkwardly posed school dance photos taken against a cheesy backdrop by a photographer that makes mildly inappropriate comments—classic.

Even though it had been years since we'd seen each other, Jeff and I easily fell back into a familiar big brother/little sister dynamic. It helped that he was pursuing an acting career as well.

"There's a nonunion audition for a play at 8 AM," Jeff said, looking up from his laptop. "Want to come with me?"

Several times a week, we woke with the sunrise to stand in line at the actor's equity building, hoping the casting directors would have time to see nonunion talent. We took turns running across the street to use the bathroom at the McDonald's and always carried the other person's headshot in our bags, just in case.

Jeff's support didn't end there. He was also the person I went to for industry advice, even though he didn't have that much more experience than I did. Still, he recognized that my eagerness to work professionally had a tendency to overrule the critical thinking necessary to choose what was best for my career—like when I booked my first "theatrical" job.

"Hell yes! What is it?" Jeff asked, giving me a bear hug.

"It's with a Renaissance fair." I paused, not wanting to tell him the rest.

"Go on . . ." Jeff was still smiling, but the corners of his mouth wavered.

"They want me to spend the day with my feet in a stockade, next to a sign inviting strangers to tickle them with a feather." I knew how ridiculous it sounded, but it was a paying job. I had done the research, I told him, and it was in fact a real role at a legitimate Ren fair.

"You're sure it's not a secret sex club?" Jeff asked, genuinely concerned. "Look, I'm not going to tell you what to do, but is that really how you want to spend the summer?"

In the end, I turned down the job offer and to this day remain grateful to Jeff for his sage advice.

Moving to New York may have meant forgoing a salaried job and benefits in favor of hustling and luck, but I was still my risk-averse father's daughter. In between auditions, I was working at the New York office of the same Boston model and talent agency I had worked at part-time during my last year of college. In Boston, I had taught acting classes to children and helped sign up "talent" the agency owner "discovered" at the mall. There hadn't been many jobs for the beautiful clients of Beantown, but I was sure the New York office would be different.

It took me one month to realize that the New York office was, in fact, also a scam. It would take another month for my conscience to get the better of me and a third to work up the courage to quit. Easily the best thing to come out of working at the agency, though, was my friendship with Jenilyn.

When I met her, Jenilyn had already been in the city for two years, having arrived shortly after earning an acting degree at a SUNY school. She knew her way around the city and was exceptionally good at having fun.

"I got us tickets to see the Canadian artist I'm obsessed with, and it's right next to that rice pudding place we wanted to try!" Hanging out with Jenilyn was exciting—more exciting than anything I would have done on my own.

"I can pay you back for the ticket, but I can't really go out afterward. I'm on a budget until I make rent." I was determined to support myself without help from my parents.

"That's okay! We'll find boys to buy us drinks, and then we won't care about spending money on rice pudding! My friend Johnny said there's a peanut butter chocolate flavor that's better than sex."

Jenilyn was a fairy of chaos and light that pulled me away from any fleeting thoughts of Ryan. "Think of how amazing the guy will be that helps you get over him!" she told me.

Around Jenilyn, only the present mattered—until we were drunk outside her apartment at 4 AM and she couldn't find her keys. Overall, we balanced each other out. Meaning I pulled her off just as many bar tops as she pulled me onto.

"How WAS YOUR date?" Jeff asked as I walked in the door.

"Well, he took me to Barnes & Noble so that he could show me all the magazines he was in, and then at the restaurant he pulled out his modeling portfolio because he wanted my 'genuine' opinion." I joined Jeff on the futon, pushing aside the sheet music he was studying.

"Ha! So when is date two?"

"Very funny."

"You need to meet the guy I'm doing this show with," Jeff said.

"You keep saying that, but you said he's not tall, *and* he's an actor. That breaks two of my established rules." It should be simple, I thought: I just wanted someone who was ambitious, tall, and not an actor. No actors, because one of us needed to have a stable income. Ambitious because I didn't need to be dragging someone along behind me, and tall because popular culture said that was important, and because I'd never dated anyone who wasn't.

"Well, I showed him your headshot, and he wants to meet you," Jeff said, smiling. Having introduced two of his friends to their now-wives, he was quite confident in his matchmaking.

"I'll meet him when I come to the show," I compromised. I knew Jeff well enough to know that he would not be letting this go.

The show was darling. It was a musical theater production of the children's book series *Henry and Mudge*, about the adventures of a seven-year-old boy and his big fluffy dog. Jeff played the dog. Eventually the show would tour to various elementary schools across the Tri-State area, but the performance that November afternoon was just a workshop in a sunlit rehearsal room, designed to further develop the production.

Jeff's mom was in town to see the show, and I had stopped to chat with her afterward when someone stepped up to introduce himself.

"Hi! Kelly, right? I'm Miguel."

Over Miguel's shoulder, I caught Jeff watching his experiment play out. Miguel was maybe five foot six, the same height as me. He had tan skin, short dark curly hair, and deep brown eyes. If he hadn't been so sweaty from bouncing around in the sweltering rehearsal room for an hour, I would have thought he was pretty cute.

"You were great in the show," I offered, and I meant it. He had an amazing voice and was obviously talented. Though admittedly watching him play a first grader had not been a wild turn-on—even if he was clearly in his twenties.

"Thanks! It's been fun to work on. And Jeff's awesome. Are you going to come out and grab a drink with us?" he asked, still sweaty, still short, still an actor.

"No, I have plans."

A for effort, Jeff, but I was finally forging my own path, and I was not about to get distracted by anyone who didn't meet my very high (pun intended) standards.

CHAPTER FIVE
The Controller

The walls around you are higher than Fort Knox," his email read.

I took it as a compliment, but was pretty sure the sender, a guy I had been on a couple dates with, didn't mean it that way. Whoever this next evolution of me was going to become, she would be strong and in control. My independence and career mattered above all else, and any vulnerability would be left for the characters I portrayed in my acting classes, not for the men I went out with.

I found a sense of control where I could, making lists of my career goals and outlining exactly what I needed to do to achieve them. While I still found some control in disordered eating, I was thankfully no longer forcing a finger down my throat or including the caloric count of diet pills in my daily total. Even on my freewheeling nights with Jenilyn, I maintained control. The course of the evening may have been unknown, but who I'd be going home with was not. With little interest in a relationship, I found great satisfaction in turning down advances.

"No, thank you!" I told the men trying to work their way between Jenilyn and me on the dance floor. And when they wouldn't stop, "I said, no thank you!"

Jenilyn cried with laughter at my polite but firm rejections. You can take the girl out of the Midwest . . .

Walking the streets of New York, I felt powerful and independent in a way I'd never experienced before. I was barely making my rent each month by hostessing and waiting tables, but I was living in New York City, supporting myself and pursuing a dream. There was this feeling when the sun hit the buildings just right, while I was navigating the crowds with the deftness of an F1 racer and the cacophony of the city started to sound like a symphony, that I couldn't believe I got to live here. In the greatest city on Earth.

It was Jenilyn's birthday, and we were out to dinner at her favorite restaurant—conveniently, an Italian spot right around the corner from my apartment. The group was finishing up in preparation for a night of drinking and dancing in Manhattan.

SOS, the text message from Jeff read.

What's wrong? I typed back on my new flip phone.

Just come home.

I told Jenilyn I would meet her at the bar and rushed through the cold January air back to our apartment. When I flung open our front door, Jeff and the guy he had done that children's show with, Miguel, were sitting on the futon watching football. No smoke, no fire, no emergency to be found.

"SOS?" I asked Jeff from the doorway.

Jeff smiled unabashedly in return. Miguel looked back and forth between us.

"I thought maybe you'd like to watch the game with us," Jeff said. He patted the space between him and Miguel on the couch.

Miguel appeared confused, apparently still unaware we were being set up. Point one for Jeff. I sighed.

"There's a group heading to a bar in Chelsea to go dancing for Jenilyn's birthday. Do you want to come?" I assumed this would bring the matter to a close. Jeff was a Nebraska boy: meat and potatoes in a T-shirt and jeans. He had little interest in hot spots with dress codes, and he certainly did not go dancing at bars serving $20 cocktails.

"Yes, yes we do!" Jeff said with a smirk. I shook my head in disbelief as he ducked behind his wall/curtain to change. His persistence was as annoying as it was admirable.

"Uh, okay, sure," Miguel responded. He pointed to his backpack by the door. "They probably won't let me bring my bag in, though."

"Leave it here, you can get it tonight or tomorrow," Jeff yelled from his room.

When the three of us arrived at the bar, we found Jenilyn surrounded by friends in a large corner booth near the back. The lighting was low, and the music was thrumming, leaving little to do but drink and dance. Jeff posted up in the red leather booth with a bottle of Budweiser. Distracted by friends and a great DJ, I forgot about Jeff's scheming until Miguel made his way over to me on the small dance floor. Miguel was a far better dancer than any of the boys I had "no, thank you'd" that night. Maybe it was the mood lighting, the three vodka cranberries, or his perfect lower lip, but my heart started doing a fluttering thing whenever Miguel and I made eye contact.

Off the dance floor, Miguel got along easily with Jenilyn's friends, even managing to chat with them over the music. There was something disarming about his presence. Despite being an actor, he wasn't a showman who demanded attention. Instead, he oozed that quiet confidence I'd recognized in Alex several years before. The fluttering feeling spread.

As the night came to a close, it was decided by someone, probably Jeff, that Miguel would come back to our apartment in Astoria. He had to get his bag after all, and he might as well sleep on our futon instead of hiking all the way back to his apartment in Harlem. On the subway ride home, drunk and happy, I flirtatiously rested my head on Miguel's shoulder. Across the train car from us, Jeff ate up every victorious minute.

Back in our apartment, still buzzing from the night, Jeff, Miguel, and I settled in front of the TV to watch a rebroadcast of *Saturday Night Live*. The boys were on the futon while I chose to sit on the floor, leaning against them both. It wasn't long before Jeff said his good nights and slipped behind the curtain that formed his wall. His work here was done.

I scooted closer to Miguel's legs, drawn by invisible forces I no longer had the desire to fight. I was pretty sure he was into me, but what if I'd read the signals wrong? Leaning my head back on the futon, I looked at him, catching his eye. He smiled but made no move toward me. I laughed absentmindedly at the TV, but my mind was far more focused on what my next move would be. The flutters had become a vibration I could feel throughout my body. I leaned back once more, this time telepathically willing him to kiss me. Whether it was the telepathy, my uncomfortable gaze, or a reciprocated desire, Miguel finally took the hint and kissed me. It was a slightly awkward, upside-down, Spider-Man style kiss—and it was perfect.

Thankfully, I was not drunk enough to forget that there was only a curtain separating Jeff from the fruits of his labor, and I moved our after-after-party to my bedroom. I woke the next morning to Miguel lying beside me.

"Good morning, beautiful," he said, his head still on the pillow.

"Good morning." It had been a while since I'd shared my bed with someone. However, instead of regretful or uncertain, I felt surprisingly relaxed. And maybe a little hungover. I stared at his face and his lower lip as he shifted onto his elbow.

"So, there's this girl," he said, looking away.

"What does that mean?" I sat up—no longer relaxed and definitely hungover.

"I kind of have a girlfriend. It only happened recently, over the holidays, because, I don't know, it was the holidays. But last night . . ." He trailed off.

"You can leave now." I picked sweatpants and a T-shirt off the floor, threw them on, and opened my bedroom door.

I watched as Miguel gathered his things, including his bag, which was still sitting by our front door. He paused and turned back to me. "I really did have a great time with you."

"Yeah," I said, swinging the door closed behind him.

"Jeff! What the fuck!" I yelled, pulling back his curtain/door/wall. "Did you know he had a girlfriend?!"

"What?" Jeff was still in bed, barely awake.

"He has a girlfriend!" I repeated.

"He never mentioned another girl to me—ever." Jeff sighed. "What an asshole."

That evening, I was making dinner when Jeff called to me from our living room.

"So, uh, Miguel just texted. He's asking for your phone number. Want me to tell him to fuck off?" he asked.

I stirred the store-bought tomato sauce I was heating on the stove and weighed my options. No matter what Miguel had to say, I still held all the power at the moment, and I quite enjoyed that feeling.

"It's okay, I'm a big girl. Give him my number." *This should be interesting.*

Not three minutes went by before my phone rang.

"Hello?" I answered, as if I didn't know exactly who was calling me.

"Hi, Kelly? It's Miguel. Jeff gave me your number."

"Yeah, he told me." Like a cat playing with a mouse.

"I just wanted to say I'm sorry for how everything went this morning and that I, um, I think you're really awesome. I know that Jeff likes to do karaoke so, uh, maybe we could all go out together sometime?"

Oh, this was too good.

"I don't really sing," I answered.

"Right, well, maybe something else then."

The whole conversation lasted all of two painfully awkward yet thoroughly enjoyable minutes before we hung up. Not finished with his punishment, I sent one last text.

Thanks for the pity/guilt call. But not necessary.

My phone rang almost immediately.

"That was not how I wanted that conversation to go." I could hear the quiet confidence easing back into his voice. "I would like to take you to dinner."

My resolve was slipping. But I had no intention of being the other woman.

"Sure thing. As soon as you don't have a girlfriend."

"Are you free Friday?"

"How about you text me when you're single, and then we can discuss dinner."

This was not how I had thought this conversation would go. But being pursued like this felt even better than the power trip I'd enjoyed minutes earlier. Still, I needed action and receipts.

By Friday, Miguel was, in fact, single. He swore he hadn't broken up with her *for* me, but *because* of me.

"If I can feel this way about someone else, then I shouldn't be in that relationship," he explained.

I cleared my throat in a way that sounded an awful lot like, "semantics."

We met for dinner at a Mexican restaurant, and before we'd even been served our entrées, he was leaning over the table asking if he could kiss me. We talked about his large Latino family in Dallas and how he was the middle of three brothers—and the only one that had left Texas. His dad was of Mexican descent, had retired early, and now spent most of his time taking care of his grandchildren.

"What about your mom?" I asked.

"She's an elementary school teacher," Miguel answered, reaching for the hot sauce.

"And what is her heritage?"

"She's white."

"Okay, but is she Irish? German?" I asked, laughing at the ambiguousness of his answer.

"Oh, I don't know—she's just white." He said, dousing his enchiladas in the hot sauce.

Miguel's performance genes had likely come from his father, who regularly sang with Miguel's tíos at family celebrations. These mini concerts were followed by skits that Miguel put on with his brothers and cousins. But it was his mother that had gotten him involved in community theater.

After attending a small Catholic elementary and middle school, he'd gone on to a very large and overcrowded public high school. That is, until he'd met Erin while doing one of those community theater shows. Erin attended Booker T. Washington High School, the performing arts magnet or *Fame* high school of Dallas, and she convinced him to transfer in as a junior. Though the acting and vocal programs were full, Miguel took an open spot in the dance program. Miguel and Erin remained friends, and she now also lived in New York. He spoke about her like a sister, and I found myself more nervous to meet her than his family (should we get that far).

"Senior year, the school had this musical theater showcase where different colleges came to watch us perform. I got offers from a few different schools, but Emerson College offered me the most money, so I went there," Miguel said.

"Seriously?! I went to college in Boston too—Northeastern. What year did you graduate?" I asked.

"'99, you?"

"I didn't start college until 2000." So he was older. That explained the confidence. "Did you like Boston?"

"Loved it, which I guess was lucky since I'd never visited before starting school," Miguel said in between bites.

"You didn't go on a campus tour or attend freshman orientation or anything?"

"We couldn't afford any of that. My first time visiting Boston was the day I moved in."

I set down my fish taco and stared at him.

"You'd never been to Boston before?"

"Nope. My parents put me and my bags on a plane, and somehow I figured out how to take the T to my dorm." Miguel shrugged. His nonchalant telling only made the story that much more wild to me.

"So you also moved into college by yourself?"

"Yeah, I guess so. I never really thought about it. I just went to college. Do you want to try these enchiladas? The mole is really good."

No tear-filled emotional goodbye with his mom and dad in his dorm room. Just an eighteen-year-old kid and his luggage, before widespread cell phone usage, navigating public transportation for the first time in his life. There is something about that image that has never left me and has helped form my elemental understanding of who Miguel is at his core: a man riding the waves of life, shifting his weight to alter the direction when he could, but mostly seeing where the water takes him. Call it luck, skill, or intuition, but I have never met anyone better at choosing the right waves to ride.

When I was with Miguel, I didn't feel just desired, but also valued. He was unassuming but confident. He held doors for me like a gentleman but spoke to me like an equal. Three days later, I was holding myself back from texting him something ridiculous like "can you get out of my head already?" But I would never, because I couldn't let on how much I liked him and thus relinquish any power I still held. I'd spent four years in a relationship feeling powerless. That is not how this one, whatever it was going to be, would start.

One date turned into several, turned into meeting each other's friends, turned into neither of us being interested in dating anyone else.

All in a matter of weeks. Our first Valentine's Day was just four weeks into dating. He made me chicken parmesan, and we watched too many episodes of *Lost* in the tiny bedroom of the apartment he shared with two roommates in Harlem.

As the relationship progressed, I was happy to let Miguel steer, as long as I remained in control of the pedals. I'd never thought of myself as a commitment-phobe, but I'd taken to referring to Miguel as "my boyfriendish person." While I liked the security and stability of relationships, I had planned my life with Ryan so much that even when I knew it wasn't right, I had struggled to edit the plans. Ironically, it wasn't that I didn't trust Miguel, it was that I didn't trust *myself* to be in another relationship.

Yet even a few months in, a smile still spontaneously appeared on my face when I saw him. The flutters I felt when we touched weren't abating. I had hopelessly fallen for the dimple lines that formed around his mouth when he smiled, his thoughtful eyes, and that damn lower lip. He never seemed to get bogged down by expectations and lists the way I did. He was forever living in the present. Sure, it got him in trouble when he lost his wallet/keys/cell phone or when he arrived fifteen minutes late to . . . just about everything. But whatever trouble he created almost always worked out in the end, and in a way that made you think it had been his plan all along. He was also twenty-nine, with his own friends, his own life, successfully pursuing his career. He didn't need me. He wanted me around because he liked being with me. Wanting is so much sexier than needing.

"I booked the *25th Annual Putnam County Spelling Bee* first national tour!" Miguel said excitedly through the phone.

"That's amazing! Congrats!" I was feigning excitement and hoped he couldn't tell. But what the actual fuck? We had been together for five months, and I was only just beginning to accept I was falling in love with a short actor who hadn't been single when we met. And then he went and booked a ten-month national tour of a Broadway musical. What an asshole. A wildly talented, charming, and ambitious asshole.

I was back home in Omaha for Cameron's high school graduation. We had family in town and were visiting the zoo. I wandered away from my family toward an alcove in the polar bear exhibit to cry. Height and profession were one thing, but I was not willing to negotiate on long-distance. The giant bears were sunning themselves on the rocks and could not have been bothered less by my relationship's impending demise.

On the flight back to New York, I was already trying to place some emotional distance between us. Would we break up when I landed? Remain together through the summer just to break up before he left? Could I handle being in a relationship that had no future?

"Let's enjoy the summer together," Miguel suggested as we lay in his lofted bed several nights later.

Neither of us were interested in long-distance, but we weren't ready to break up either. While I was enduring flashbacks to Ryan's untamed jealousy, Miguel had heard stories of the antics and escapades touring castmates got up to together and wanted to keep his options open. We agreed to break up at the end of the summer.

Haha, just kidding! Two months later, we were both hopelessly in love.

From my standpoint, Miguel had shown me what it looked and felt like to be trusted. From Miguel's, well, he had discovered that the cast was made up of mostly married folks and gay men. I would also like to think that he had fallen for my irresistible charm.

As scared as I was, I knew this long-distance relationship would be different. Miguel was not going to accuse me of cheating on him if I missed his call or expect me to leave a bar or party to talk to him. In fact, Miguel had never once yelled at me or tried to pick a fight. I was actually the one who had those bases covered.

"I'm meeting up with Erin for a drink tonight. Want to come?" Miguel asked as he walked me to the train from his apartment, a cup of coffee from the corner bodega in one hand and my hand in the other.

"I made plans with Courtney. I haven't seen her in weeks," I answered.

"But you can see her as much as you want when I'm gone," he said, partly teasing but maybe a little serious. Miguel was leaving in a couple of weeks, and the pressure to spend as much time together was mounting as our days in the same city dwindled.

"I'm allowed to have friends too!" I snapped, pulling my hand away.

"Why do you do that?" Miguel asked, stopping to face me. "You get mad instead of having a conversation about it."

"Well, I want to see you, but I have other friends to spend time with also," I said defensively.

"Right, I get that, I'm not saying you shouldn't. You just didn't have to say it that way." He reached for my hand, and we continued walking to the train.

Like water through a gorge, Ryan's patterns had cut into my psyche, defining my emotional responses. What frustrated me was that I knew what a healthy relationship looked like: my parents had modeled one. But after years of destructive behavior, I guess I forgot. Miguel reminded me there was another way. That with trust, self-love, and a little more patience than I'd ever romantically received or given, I could fill in the crevices and canyons left behind.

I can't blame my hot-headedness entirely on Ryan—part of it is who I am. I like winning, and I hate being wrong. But I also love learning and striving to be better, and Miguel was helping me grow into a better person. I hoped I was doing the same for him.

A few days before Miguel left for the tour, I met him at his apartment after a late restaurant shift. He had been out with friends and was quite drunk.

Laying in bed and sensing his vulnerability, I asked, "Mig, do you think I could be 'the one'?"

"Yes," he answered without hesitation. Then he returned the question.

"I'm too young to think about things like that." *And not nearly drunk enough to answer truthfully.*

"Then why did you ask me?" He was flustered and maybe a little embarrassed.

"I guess I didn't need to. I just wanted to confirm what I saw in your eyes. They were extra googly tonight."

He was asleep moments later and wouldn't remember the conversation in the morning. I would never forget it.

CHAPTER SIX
The Ingenue

Great news: it turns out that when you trust and support each other, long-distance is not a relationship death sentence. For ten months, we spoke on the phone nearly every day, and once every four to six weeks I would visit Miguel in whatever city the tour was currently playing. Each time I saw him was like a mini vacation where we explored a new city, ate at fun restaurants, and thoroughly enjoyed his hotel room.

I knew one of the only reasons this was maintainable, though, was because the tour had an end date. This was for now, not forever. Best yet, while we were building a foundation for our relationship, I still got to enjoy New York City *and* didn't have to deal with the self-imposed pressure of having to date anyone!

In between auditions for Culligan water softener commercials and photo shoots as the young mom in Babies "R" Us print ads, I was waiting tables at a restaurant called The Diner. It was a trendy spot with New York prices where I regularly waited on folks like Molly Shannon, who liked to come for brunch with her daughter, or Nigel Barker, whose photography studio was nearby.

The night shifts, on the other hand, served slightly less inhibited guests. Because many of the bars and clubs in Manhattan close at 4 AM and The Diner was open until 6 AM, it was a hotspot for partyers to grab disco fries or a milkshake in the early morning hours while waiting for the evening's cocaine to wear off. It helped that The Diner was in the Meatpacking District, which was undergoing a revitalization at the time. What had once been the home of meatpacking warehouses as well as a hub for sex workers was now home to fashion houses and a brand-new Apple store. While the meatpacking plants had relocated to Brooklyn or Jersey, the sex workers had stayed put.

The music was blaring but not loudly enough to cover the sounds of at least one person having an amazing time in The Diner's downstairs bathroom. I really just needed to pee before heading home on the subway.

"Oh, I saw one of the regular girls take someone in there," my coworker yelled at me as she headed up the stairs to deliver a bowl of mac 'n' cheese with chorizo. "She shouldn't be too long, but you can try sweet-talking the bouncer next door into using their bathroom."

"Gotcha, thank you!" I yelled after her. One sweet smile to the bouncer later, and I was finally hovering over a toilet seat. I was quite proud of myself for navigating a situation that would have been otherworldly to me only a few years earlier.

Unfortunately, confidence is often short-lived in New York City. Just when I would start to feel like a New Yorker, I'd accidentally take a train in the wrong direction or have a run-in with an aggressive catcaller. However, nothing would test my newfound confidence more than the entertainment industry I yearned to be a part of. Particularly the agents and casting directors.

"You're twenty-four? If you were going to make it you would have already."

"There's nothing really special about you, is there?"

"Your face is in New York and your nose is in New Jersey."

If only it had been just words.

It was an unusually warm late fall day, and I had taken the train to 72nd & Broadway for an audition. I was wearing a denim miniskirt and T-shirt and carrying a large purse that held everything I would need for the rest of the day, since I wouldn't be returning home until after my dinner shift that night.

"Excuse me!" a man's voice shouted in my direction.

I slowed my New York F1 walking pace, unwilling to stop entirely in case it was another asshole telling me to smile more, and looked over my shoulder. Behind me, a tall, overweight man with male-pattern baldness was waving at me. He seemed to be in his fifties or sixties. His overall appearance was unkempt, but his clothes looked expensive, reminiscent of the Penguin from Batman but taller.

"Are you an actress?" he yelled.

I stopped and turned. Everyone has heard the stories of being discovered on the street, of a chance meeting that changes your life.

"I am . . ." I answered. I was interested but still cautious. More than one customer at The Diner had tried to pick me up by telling me they were a casting director or knew someone who knew someone.

"I'm James Toback." He paused to see if the name meant anything to me. It didn't. "I'm a writer and director. Did you see *Bugsy? The Harvard Man?*" He spoke quickly and with purpose.

"Yes," I lied.

"Look me up, those are mine. I'm working on a new project, and I think you would be perfect for it."

He gave me a business card, and I gave him my headshot and résumé in return.

Later that night, a quick internet search told me that he was in fact who he said he was, and Academy Award–nominated at that. I accepted his offer to meet him for dinner at an Italian restaurant in the Upper West Side a couple days later. I couldn't believe my luck—a true New York moment.

After telling the restaurant's host who I was there to meet, he led me to the back of the dimly lit restaurant. Mr. Toback was sitting alone at a large table finishing up a plate of pasta. He acknowledged my presence with a nod, but did not get up to greet me. I had thought we would be dining together, but I must have misinterpreted the invitation.

"I watched *The Harvard Man*," I said, attempting small talk. "What an incredible script."

"It's a true story, inspired by an acid trip I had in college," he said matter-of-factly, then added to a passing server, "Have Leo add this to my tab."

And with that, he stood up and started walking toward the front of the restaurant. "We'll head to my office. It's just across the street." He barely even glanced back to see if I was following him.

On the short walk to his office, he dished about his famous friends, from Warren Beatty to Alec Baldwin, who he could "call right now" if I asked him to. I recognized name-dropping when I heard it, but it was hard not to be impressed. He was a legitimate writer and director; of course his friends were famous.

The building he took me to was nondescript, though notably residential. This might have raised my suspicions, except I knew many people rented apartments to use as office space in New York.

"This place was my mother's, but now I use it as my office," Toback said as if reading my mind.

When the elevator opened, Toback led me past several doors to other units before using a key to unlock a heavy door near the end. Inside was a studio apartment with a desk and chair in front of a window and, in the center of the room, a large bed.

"Have a seat," he instructed. There were papers and clothing covering every surface—except the bed. Red flags blinded my vision. But what if I was overreacting? Between my community theater childhood and being a theater kid in high school, I'd been labeled as overdramatic early and often. Was I really going to walk away from a once-in-a-lifetime opportunity because I was a little uncomfortable?

Toback walked around to the opposite side of the bed and sat down, forcing me to turn around and sit fully on the bed with my back to the door.

"I've only just begun to write this next project, but when I saw you the other day, I couldn't get you out of my head. I jerked off thinking about you several times that day. I never cum multiple times from thinking of someone I've only seen in passing." He meant this as a compliment, but I felt exposed and powerless.

"You could be my muse, but you will have to trust me. Do you trust me?"

His eyes bored into me as he waited for a response.

"I– I don't know. I don't really know you," I answered, evading the question and his gaze.

"If we're going to work together, you will have to trust me fully. As if I am God." He proceeded to list the names of other famous actresses he had worked with and who trusted him. Some of whom he claimed to have slept with. "Do you trust me?" he repeated.

I may have been naive, but I wasn't dumb. It was now perfectly clear what he hoped to get out of this "meeting." What I didn't know was whether there was still a movie on the line too. I know that sounds crazy, but I was twenty-four and desperate for a break—and James Toback was preying on that.

"I bet I would trust you by the time we started production on the movie," I offered, steering the conversation back to the reason *I* was there.

"Would you do nude scenes?" he asked.

"Depends on the scenes," I answered.

"I'd have to see you without your clothes to decide if that's what I wanted. Do you shave your pussy?" His expression went from casual, if sexually charged, to carnal. In that moment, I understood that if this was what it took for an actress to get a break, then I didn't want it badly enough. Even with my fight-or-flight response raging, even as I began to calculate an exit strategy, I was berating myself for not being willing to go further to make my dreams come true.

"I'm not answering that." I moved to get off the bed and Toback followed, positioning his heavyset six-foot frame between me and the only way out. We were several floors up, and I hadn't heard even the dulled sound of a television coming from behind any of the doors we'd passed. In this city of eight million people, I was on my own.

"I thought you said you were going to trust me," he said, stepping closer to me. My instinct to step away from him had me back against the bed. "I'll have my driver take you home, but you can't leave me like this." He pointed to his bulging pants. "You don't even have to do anything, just sit on the bed."

He proceeded to kneel in front of me and began humping my leg like a dog. I tried to look away, but he insisted that he could only cum if I squeezed his nipples and looked into his eyes. Wanting this to be over as quickly as possible, and fearing what would happen if I didn't, I did as I was told.

When he finished, he called his driver and insisted on escorting me to the elevator.

"I've killed a man," Toback bragged as we waited for the elevator. "Was never even a suspect for the crime."

The elevator doors finally opened, and I stepped inside.

"I'll call you," he said as the doors slid closed.

Outside, a black car was waiting. The driver nodded to let me know he was there for me.

"I'm in Astoria," I told the driver from the backseat. I had been so eager to get out of the apartment that it wasn't until we were halfway over the Queensboro Bridge that I realized Toback would now know where I lived. I texted Jenilyn from the car letting her know what time I should be home and that I needed her to come to my apartment as soon as possible. Then, to be safe, I had the driver drop me off a block away from my apartment.

Soaked in shame, I didn't want Jeff to hear what had happened, so I sat with Jenilyn on the stoop outside my apartment as I recounted the evening to her. How could I have been so stupid? How could I have allowed this to happen? Did this count as cheating? If Miguel found out, would he blame me? Break up with me? Jenilyn listened judgment-free and kept my secret for years.

It never occurred to me to report the incident. I was so certain it was somehow my fault for allowing myself to be in such a vulnerable situation, for allowing him to do what he did, that instead, I buried the memory and vowed it would never happen again. But that wouldn't prevent me from beginning to experience debilitating anxiety before walking into auditions. I blamed it on the pressure I put on myself, how badly I wanted to succeed, and yes, that was part of it. But I realize now that a reflexive trauma response probably had something to do with it as well.

BETWEEN HUSTLING FOR acting work and waiting tables, I was counting down the days until my next little vacation to see Miguel. From Atlanta to Orlando to Seattle and St. Louis, I always looked forward not just to seeing Miguel but also to the escape from New York. The once-sparkling city had lost some of its luster. In some ways, I suppose, so had I.

When the tour made its way to Dallas, Miguel invited me to fly down and meet his family. The *whole* family. Miguel's mother, aunt, and cousin picked me up from the airport. They were welcoming and talkative, easily calming any nervousness I felt. When I was introduced to several dozen of his tías, tíos, and primos in the lobby of the theater the following night, the excitement and pride they felt for their Miguelito was palpable. It would take me years to sort out who belonged to who and how everyone was connected, but from the start they treated me as if I was connected to them too—already a part of the family.

With multiple state lines between us, Miguel and I connected via phone conversations in a way we might not have had we been physically together and distracted by work, events, and each other's bodies. But rarely did we speak about a future together. We were both cautious, but with the end of the tour in sight, I had questions. Well, really, one question.

"So are you going to move back into the Harlem apartment when the tour is over?" I asked.

"I guess so?" Miguel answered, as if he hadn't been thinking about this as obsessively as I had.

"The lease on my apartment with Jeff is coming up not long after you get back. Would it be crazy to move in together?" I wanted to be cool, but I'm not, so I kept talking. "It's just that Harlem is so far away from Astoria, and it would really be easier if we didn't have to travel back and forth. But it has to be a two-bedroom in case we break up and I need to get a roommate." While I'd couched the pitch in practicality, my motivation could not have been further from rational thought. I was madly in love, and after ten months apart, I wanted nothing more than to wake up beside Miguel every day.

When I'd finally shut up, Miguel answered, "Yeah, that makes sense. Where should we look?"

Like the good daughter I am, I ran the idea by my parents. Mom said that we should absolutely move in together. "How else will you know if you can live with him when you're married?" Ever practical, but also—woah, Mom, we're living together, not registering for wedding china we'd never use. Dad didn't love the idea, but he gave his blessing as long as I didn't tell my conservative great-aunts.

So Miguel and I found an apartment in Astoria on the second floor of a traditional three-story, six-unit, Queens brownstone. It even had two real bedrooms, no curtain needed, just in case. Though, my favorite part was the sun-washed front stoop, which was perfect for people-watching while enjoying bagels and coffee on Sunday mornings.

After buying furniture that was entirely too big for the apartment, we celebrated by throwing a "Living in Sin" party—which was really just a housewarming party with a fun name where we played Guitar Hero and Mario Kart. But also a cathartic fuck-you to the girls at the high school slumber party that told me I was going to hell if I had sex before marriage.

I doubt that any of them remember that slumber party shaming, knew about my current living situation, or even gave a shit. But after a decade of being told how sexual I should be, what my body should look like, and what I should do with it to please others, taking back control in this small way felt damn good. Being an ingenue may be sweet, but owning my autonomy was so much sweeter.

CHAPTER SEVEN
The Luckiest

After three years trying to make it in New York, I started spinning out under self-applied pressure. I was sneaking diet pills again, and there was no question I dreaded hearing more than what I'd been up to lately—which I always interpreted as a question about my career and not my general life. I was almost twenty-six and working steadily as an actress and commercial print model, but not enough to quit the security of my restaurant job or to feel fulfilled by the work I was booking. The New York City hustle, which had originally been energizing, now felt like a rat race on a hamster wheel. Miguel was the only part of my life that felt secure or stable.

One frigid night, the two of us were walking from the subway to our apartment after drinks with friends, me clinging to Miguel less for warmth and more to keep my balance on the icy sidewalks. Comforted by Miguel's steady arm and uninhibited by the evening's libations, I blurted out, "If you proposed, I would say yes."

"That's good to know," Miguel replied as if I'd just shared the weather report.

The next morning, I awoke in a panic at the memory of my ine-briated declaration. It wasn't that I didn't want to marry Miguel—I couldn't imagine meeting anyone else that I would rather spend my life with. But I did *not* want to still be serving hamburgers and disco fries to intoxicated assholes while wearing Mimi's ring on my finger. I had hoped to have life a little more figured out, or at least be fully support-ing myself with acting work.

Mimi's ring, the one Mom and Dad had given me in college, was tucked in the back of my nightstand, and I was pretty sure Miguel knew exactly where to find it. Later that afternoon, while Miguel was in the shower, I re-hid the ring in the bottom of a sweater box under our bed. If he couldn't find it, he couldn't propose, right?

SINCE HIGH SCHOOL, whenever I've felt out of control, Courtney has been there to inject a dose of rationality into my life. When I needed a break from Ryan or roommate drama, I had visited Courtney at the college she attended just outside Boston. She remained a grounding force in New York as well and always had an interesting or artsy event to invite me to. That week, it was the screening of a documentary about Ethiopian women affected by obstetric fistulas and the dedi-cated medical professionals working to provide them with care and support. So not a real mood lifter, but it was a sobering reminder of all I took for granted.

Exiting the theater, surrounded by the gleaming apartments and designer stores of Greenwich Village, there was no way to avoid New York City's apathetic affluence. I felt accosted by the vast disparities between the Ethiopian women's access to care, opportunity, and dig-nity with my own. My scope of the world was narrow, and my life's purpose had become consumed by what I thought success looked like. In any cosmopolitan city, but especially New York, it was easy to get caught up in *Vogue*'s September issue, 40 under 40 lists, and Page Six. Art, flavor, and culture are important, but I had lost the ability to identify the tipping point between meaningful and frivolous. While I was tearing myself apart in a quest for status and success, the film confronted me with the far harsher reality of many other peoples' lives—people who'd been thrown into motherhood before their bodies were ready, who suffered years of physical pain and social ostracization, and who had overcome extreme obstacles to reach the medical care they needed.

A typical response to such a realization might have involved sharing the documentary on social media and making a plea for others to be aware of the issue. Perhaps hosting a fundraiser to benefit a fistula hospital. Or maybe even getting involved with a maternal medicine nonprofit closer to home. All would have been empathetic and sensible responses.

Instead, I went home and researched the fistula hospital in the documentary to see if they took volunteers.

Look, no one has ever accused me of thinking too small. Discovering their volunteers needed to have a medical background (duh . . .) didn't deter me, though. Maybe there was another way I could contribute, perhaps through education or empowering girls to advocate for themselves and build independent futures. I began researching organizations in the region that *were* looking for regular ol' nonmedical volunteers.

"I found an orphanage in Tanzania that is accepting volunteers, and I am going to go for a month this summer," I informed Miguel and my parents that spring. "Before you freak out, Tanzania is a relatively safe place to travel so you won't need to worry." How thoughtful of me to offer reassurances about a country I knew almost nothing about.

Even though my heart was in the right place, the white saviorism of my actions now makes me cringe. In time, I would learn to channel what I witnessed in Tanzania into more meaningful and sustainable contributions, but back then I'm not sure I would have even listened to anyone who tried to teach me about effective community support. Right or wrong, this trip was about helping myself break out of the monotonous cycle I found myself in as much or even more than it was about helping others.

Mom and Dad had banked on Miguel joining me, but he had accepted a job reprising his role as Chip Tolentino in a regional production of *The 25th Annual Putnam County Spelling Bee* in Pittsfield, Massachusetts.

"I'm coming with you," Mom told me, days after learning I had every intention of embarking on this transcontinental adventure alone.

"Mom, I don't think you'd like it. I'm staying at the orphanage, not a hotel or even a hostel," I replied in disbelief. When Mom had been my Girl Scout troop leader in elementary school, she had taken us "camping" at a hotel where she helped us earn our Looking Your Best badge and then driven us to the outlet mall to earn a Consumer Power badge. She was not often found outside of her narrow comfort zone.

"I'm not going to be able to sleep the entire time you are away, so I might as well join you." There was no arguing with her.

As if trying to distract myself from my emotional instability with a month-long trip halfway across the world wasn't enough, I also convinced Miguel that this would be a great time for us to get a puppy. So three months before I boarded a plane to Arusha, Tanzania, we drove a rental car to New Jersey where a sweet grandmother was selling a litter of cockapoo puppies. By the time we got there, only two of the pups remained. I wasn't sure how we would choose, but when one of them began moonwalking backward before pissing on the floor, I knew he was the one.

"What should we name him?" I asked Miguel as we carried him to the rental car.

"Well, he has a little red in his fur. How about Tabasco?" my hot sauce–loving boyfriend suggested.

"Ha! I like it. Welcome to our little family, Tabasco."

Though he was kept pretty busy training Tabasco, who followed him everywhere, Miguel offered to throw me a benefit concert to help offset the cost of my trip (which I couldn't even remotely afford). Or rather, I would plan it, and he and some friends would perform. I reserved the second floor of our favorite Irish pub in midtown Manhattan and invited everyone I'd ever met in New York.

Miguel, along with his *Spelling Bee* tour friends, put together a Ben Folds Five cover band and played for fifty or so of our friends who showed up in support. They jammed away to "One Angry Dwarf," "Kate," and "Rockin' the Suburbs." Then, halfway through "The Luckiest," Miguel dropped to one knee, pulled Mimi's ring out of his jeans pocket, and asked me to marry him.

"Yes! Yes! Yes!" I answered through tears, holding his face and kissing him as our friends cheered around us. "But how did you find the ring?"

"I ransacked our whole apartment while you were at the store this afternoon," he said, smiling.

Call it luck or divine intervention, but minutes before I came home, he'd found the ring box tucked between the folds of my sweaters.

AFTER ALL THE effort Miguel had taken to find the ring, I decided it was probably safer to leave it behind on my transatlantic journey. I wasn't the only one leaving something behind. At Good Hope Orphanage in Arusha, Tanzania, Mom went the longest she ever has, and likely ever will, without doing her hair or makeup.

"It is actually quite freeing," she confessed, "but I don't plan on making a habit of it."

We helped with meal prep, did dishes, taught in the orphanage's school, painted walls, and played with the children. We slept in sleeping bags on cots, went to the bathroom over toilets that you had to pour water into to flush, and washed ourselves with a bucket of water heated over an open flame.

The aunties and teachers who oversaw the orphanage and school were welcoming but not shy about putting us to work. They made sure chores were completed and a routine was followed. However, there was also always time to play and dance. The children were loved and well cared for—most importantly, they were happy. It must have been so difficult for them to grow attached to the orphanage volunteers only to have them leave over and over again, especially after whatever trauma had separated them from their families in the first place.

Every few days, there were a couple hours of downtime where we could write home, wash our dust-filled clothes in metal basins, or go into Arusha to explore or visit the internet cafés. The aunties would not hear of us going into town on our own and enlisted Bakari or Mohammad, two of the teenage boys who hung around the orphanage doing odd jobs, to be our chaperones. Thankfully, the boys were eager to practice their English, and we got along well. In between rudimentary Kiswahili lessons, I loved listening to whatever they were willing to share about their daily lives.

From Bakari and Mohammad, I learned how difficult it was to attend secondary school, i.e., junior high and high school. For starters, there are fees associated with public secondary school, so many students couldn't afford to continue with their education. Mohammad was incredibly excited to be starting secondary school that fall, but Bakari had not been able to enroll.

And yet even without things like education access and electricity guaranteed to them, the people I met during my time at the orphanage were by far more content than many of the people I knew back home. I don't wish to minimize the economic, medical, technological, and educational hurdles they experience—obviously Bakari would have much preferred to be attending school with Mohammad. But he and my other Tanzanian friends were able to find joys that I and my immensely privileged American social circle would have completely overlooked. It slowly dawned on me that we weren't just using different units of measure to qualify our lives and happiness; we weren't even measuring the same things. Living in Tanzania, and learning about peoples' lives and value systems there, put a tiny crack in my own lifelong American value system. I began to ask myself, When is more just more? And how do we establish the deeply personal difference between settling and accepting? I didn't have the answers, but to be fair I'd only just learned to ask the questions.

The day we left for home, the aunties gave us hugs and thanked us for coming. Then they returned to caring for the children and preparing lunch. New volunteers would arrive, and life would go on. Conversely, I don't think I stopped crying until we landed at our first layover in Nairobi. I was distraught at not knowing when or if I would ever be able to return to this beautiful country and the people I now cared so much about. My world had been rocked. For the wonderful people of Good Hope Orphanage, it was simply Saturday.

Up to that point, I had spent most of my life trying to control as many variables as possible so that I could achieve the most optimal outcomes, rendering me special. But special as measured by what? Awards? Accolades? How well-known I was? Even if I achieved everything my heart desired, even if I finally felt like I had lived up to my "special" potential, I would never be more or less special than any other person on the planet. We were all just living out the lives we were born into, whether we saw cement and skyscrapers before us or dirt roads and baobab trees.

Upon returning to New York, I met up with a friend who had been to Uganda not long before I went to Tanzania. We had both been profoundly moved by the lack of access to secondary school, and together we formed a nonprofit to sponsor East African kids and teens in their education. We held a few fundraisers and were able to begin sponsoring Bakari's education. After the foundation folded, I still made sure, through personal gifts and donations from family and friends, to continue to support Bakari.

As for Bakari himself, he was able to finish secondary school and went on to earn a tourism degree. Today, he owns and operates

Kadogoo, an experiential travel company that includes a hostel and a safari tour service as well as volunteer and internship experiences. He also started his own NGO, Progress for Africa, which runs a neighborhood primary school and provides income to women in the community by hiring them to manage a large chicken coop.

And I want to be very clear: this was all Bakari's doing, not mine. He put in the thought, the time, and the hard work. I just helped with access. The impact he has made on his community is undeniably so much greater than whatever some resource-full volunteer from a developed nation could have done. If nothing else, that is what my time in Tanzania taught me: that real change doesn't come from volunteers swooping in—it comes from local leaders like Bakari, who know what their communities need. I'm grateful to have played a small role in supporting his journey, even if the most important thing I could do was step back and cheer from afar.

IN ADDITION TO a few souvenirs and hundreds of photos, I had also returned from Tanzania with a new perspective and a freshly installed bullshit filter. Life felt clearer, decisions more obvious. Which was convenient, considering I now had many decisions to make with Miguel regarding our upcoming nuptials.

We were finalizing details for a September wedding when Michael Mayer, the director of a new show called *The Untitled Punk Rock Musical*, called. Miguel had been a part of a few early workshops, but now the show was getting an out-of-town run in Berkeley, California, and they wanted Miguel to be a part of it.

"I hear the Bay Area is beautiful for fall weddings," Michael told Miguel.

We were, in fact, not planning a Bay Area wedding, and had already put down a deposit on a venue in Westchester, NY. Thankfully, the venue still had one weekend date available that summer: the Fourth of July. After an incredibly rainy start to the summer, we were married on the first sunny weekend of the season. A mariachi band played while we danced up the aisle as husband and wife and continued through the cocktail hour, during which guests were informed that, in lieu of wedding favors, a donation had been made to Good Hope Orphanage in their honor.

Our first dance was to "The Luckiest," sung by one friend and accompanied by another. With every spin on the dance floor, I could see my old roommate Jeff's victorious shit-eating grin. There wasn't a dry eye in the house as Miguel's father gave a speech about two ships meeting in a harbor, and I am forever indebted to my cousin, who helped clean up a freshly twenty-one-year-old Cameron after he took a few too many shots with my uncles. Then, once the sun had set, the private golf course next door to our venue lit up the sky with a brilliant complimentary firework display. Surrounded by family and friends, watching fireworks in the arms of my husband, I had never felt luckier in my life.

THE DAY AFTER we returned from our honeymoon, Miguel was off to Berkeley, California. *The Untitled Punk Rock Musical* became Green Day's *American Idiot*, and several months after its Northern California debut, the production exploded onto the stage at New York's St. James Theatre in the spring of 2010. To date, it remains one of my favorite Broadway shows.

Behind the scenes, life was imitating art imitating life imitating art. The party-hard, punk rock rebellion occurring onstage wasn't ending when the curtain came down. The members of Green Day, with Billie Joe Armstrong at the helm, enmeshed themselves in the production. They invited the cast to perform alongside them at the Grammys, held late-night concerts (really, parties) in small seedy music venues, and often continued the festivities with after-parties and after-after-parties. Omaha Kelly would have been equal parts starstruck and scandalized.

Seeing Miguel experience such a career high forced a reckoning with my own. For five years, I had hustled, prioritizing my career above all else, and I had found some success: national print campaigns, a slew of commercials, and a few small TV roles. There had also been play readings, in-house corporate videos, independent films, and one international music video. I was working more than I had at any other point in my career, but it still wasn't enough to live off. Nor did it provide for reliable health insurance, which we would need before Miguel and I even thought about starting a family.

I got a high from each job I booked, but that high was lasting for a shorter and shorter amount of time. Afterward, the withdrawal symptoms would set in: I grew insecure and depressed, having to force myself up from the bottom of the tub at the end of my showers. I knew this wasn't healthy, but how do you give up a dream? And if I somehow found the strength, what would I even do next?

When I got back from Tanzania, I never returned to my job at The Diner. Thankfully, Miguel's best friend from high school, Erin, was hiring. Following her dancing career, she had made a name for herself in the New York hospitality scene, going from the food and beverage director of an exclusive members-only club to the director of operations of a new Michelin-starred restaurant across from Central Park. In between auditions, I worked as her assistant, helping with reservations and learning basic restaurant operations.

By the time Miguel and I were married, Erin had moved on to *Top Chef* host Tom Colicchio's newest venture. Riverpark was a massive restaurant with an even larger event space. It was beautifully situated overlooking the East River, with massive glass windows and an outdoor patio. Initial efforts had focused on getting the main dining room open, but when that was finished and Erin started organizing the events department, she took a leap of faith and asked me to join her.

"What do I tell Erin about this job?" I asked Miguel.

We were sitting backstage at the St. James Theatre, in a crew office where the abundance of beer bottles and chicken wing boxes more closely resembled the floor of a fraternity house than that of a Broadway theater office. When I was free on Sundays, I would stop by the theater in between the matinee and evening performances to watch football with Miguel and his buddies.

"What's the job?" Andrew, Miguel's friend and castmate, asked me while cracking open a beer for me.

"Not an acting one. I'd be working for Mig's friend at a new restaurant on the East Side, coordinating and selling events. It's like a *job* job." I made a face at the thought of working at a desk, answering phones and emails.

"Like with a salary and benefits and consistency? Take it! I would," Andrew said before turning his attention back to the game.

"Says the asshole on Broadway . . ." I threw a balled-up napkin at the back of his head.

Miguel sat silently next to me. I knew he would never tell me to give up acting, but he was one of the few people in my life who saw the toll the industry was taking on me. My dream was harming me more than driving me, but giving it up felt like a betrayal to the little girl I had once been, the one that dreamed of being special and had eventually learned to redraw the lines of her life, allowing her to pursue her dream.

Since then, from more than twenty years of being in or adjacent to the entertainment industry, I've learned that it's not a question of *if* someone leaves the business but *when*. Eventually, most performers move into other fields, be they teaching, production, or something else wholly unrelated. One friend became a financial advisor, another went back to school to be a therapist, another opened a bakery. This isn't failure. It is an understanding that the demands of the accompanying lifestyle no longer fit their priorities and life goals. I didn't know that at the time though. What I did know was that I was exceedingly lucky that my next career move just happened to fall into my lap.

In an ironic twist, I would get more use out of my acting classes as I sold and negotiated events than I ever did on a commercial set. I learned to watch, listen, and match my event clients the way I would a scene partner. I was still inherently myself, but I would flavor my performances to meet the moment. Dad was thrilled that I was finally using the college degree he'd paid for, and I loved reminding him that it was the acting classes *I* had paid for that were proving more useful.

I kept waiting to miss performing, to be jealous of Miguel's opportunities—but it turns out I really enjoyed having responsibility, a salary, and health insurance. It also helped that I was really good at this job: details, lists, managing multiple moving parts while competing to meet sales goals? Check, check, and check. The hours were long, and tensions often ran high, but I felt in control of my work and growth in a way I was never able to as an actress.

Even though I didn't miss acting, I did miss my big dreams and atypical lifestyle. In my journal several months into the new job I wrote, "What do I dream of now?"

For better or worse, I wouldn't have much time to miss dreaming. A year into the new job, and a few months after *American Idiot* throttled the St. James for the last time, Miguel and I were crying over a pregnancy test on our kitchen counter.

I wanted to be one of the expectant mothers who glowed and crooned over the miracle of life growing inside her, but mostly I felt swollen, gassy, and like the baby was trying to push me out of my own body. Miguel, however, was beside himself with excitement. For most of my second trimester, he was in Dallas, doing an out-of-town run of a show called *Giant*, which had aspirations of transferring to New York.

"I know we can't be together, but we will be very soon. Here's your present! I love you," Miguel said in a Valentine's Day video message before picking up his guitar and singing a song he had written. It ended with the following lyrics:

And as the years go by,
A new arrival will start to cry.
We'll never be the same,
He'll have your eyes, and he'll share my name.
I've never felt like this before,
Wanna knock on every door,
Shout and yell so all will know,
We have so far yet to go,
There's nothing that we cannot do,
I'm the luckiest because of you.

CHAPTER EIGHT
The Mother

Until I met Miguel, I wasn't entirely sure if I wanted to be a mother. Had my career taken off and I met a man who didn't want children, I was fairly certain I would have been okay without them. But if we all have some deeper purpose to our lives, a reason to exist, then Miguel's was to be a father. I saw it when he was with his niece and nephew, or in the same room with an infant—whether he knew the parents or not. He lit up around children and they around him. He was going to be an incredible father, and he gave me the confidence to add motherhood to my list of life goals.

And now here I was with a plump baby swaddled on the couch next to me. He lay there like a bound slug, wrapped tightly, but not too tight, just the right tight, like they had taught me to do in the new parents' class at the hospital. I spotted a loose corner of the muslin cloth, one that I had pre-laundered months before I'd squeezed Jackson's eight-pound, six-ounce frame out of my body, and tucked it back into place. I examined his face, searching for a connection, a feeling, a . . . something. Whatever it was, it wasn't there.

We had now been together for three days on this side of my uterus. He ate, burped, slept, pooped, peed, cried, and stared at me. A stare far more intense than any few-days-old child should be able to maintain. To anyone watching, I was playing the role of doting mother quite successfully: reading the books, singing the songs, taking the pictures. But it felt like pretend, like a staged play with a postnatal audience of one.

I definitely cared about this tiny human; he was adorable, and I marveled at the tininess of each body part—but I wasn't in love with him. It terrified me to admit this, even if only to myself. Weren't mothers supposed to be enamored with their baby at first glance? Awash in maternal glow and protection? Bound to them by some unspeakable force of nature? If so, I had somehow skipped that page of his birth story.

"It's all a little anticlimactic, isn't it?" Miguel commented on our second night at home.

"What do you mean?" I feigned confusion, but I was secretly craving this honest opening. Tabasco nestled in closer to me. He had fully switched allegiances from Miguel to me during the pregnancy, perhaps sensing a rival for my attention.

"It's just that there is all this excitement and anxiety leading up to the baby . . . and then they're here, and it just is what it is. We pour all of ourselves into keeping him alive and in return he just lays there."

The diligent mommy role I was playing wanted to defend our precious offspring, but the real me, the sleep-deprived and emotional me, just couldn't.

"Do you think it's normal to need some time to fall in love with him?" I asked. "For it not to be an instantaneous thing?"

"It took us time to fall in love with each other. It makes sense that it might take us some time to fall in love with him too."

The relief I felt at Miguel's reasoning wouldn't completely wash away my guilt, but it tempered it. Whether my disconnect was due to hormones, exhaustion, or me simply needing time to emotionally and physically recalibrate, I'll never know for sure. But over the next few weeks, a love stronger and more feral than anything I had ever experienced began to take hold of my heart until it felt like its sole purpose was to beat for this dependent creature. By the time I returned to work just two months later (restaurants are not exactly known for their maternity leave policies), my daily reunification with Jackson could not come soon enough. The way his face lit up when he heard my voice—even if it was only because he knew he was about to get his dinner straight from the milk source—was everything I never knew I needed.

IT WASN'T LONG before Miguel was dreaming out loud of leaving the city. I understood why: Jackson's toys had taken over our apartment, we used a rolling duffle bag to carry our groceries home, and now that Jackson was seven months old, I was struggling to carry him and his stroller up and down the stairs of the subway. But I was terrified of returning to the homogenous suburbs of my youth.

"Life doesn't have to be this hard," Mom said during one visit as she watched me pack up multiple loads of laundry to take to our corner laundromat. "Why not consider moving out of the city?"

"I have it under control," I replied, stopping to pick up a onesie that had fallen out of the laundry bag. "And if we move out of the city, my commute would be longer. Then I'd get even less time with Jackson."

I knew suburban life would be easier in so many ways, but plenty of people raised children in the city; why couldn't we? Miguel was persistent, though. He wanted more space, a yard, a car, and a driveway to park it in.

"The house has to be in walking distance from the train station, have three bedrooms and a big yard for Jackson and Tabasco, and be within our price range," I told him, certain I was buying time because there was no way we could get it all.

Miguel found our home the first day he took the train to New Jersey to look.

It was a sweet, yellow, 1,100-square-foot ranch house in Maplewood, New Jersey, a forty-minute train ride from New York City. It had a massive backyard and was a ten-minute walk to the train station, the adjacent "downtown" village, and a beautiful park with ballfields and a woodchip-strewn playground.

When the mortgage company informed us the house would need to be purchased based on my income exclusively because Miguel's was too erratic, Miguel grinned and said, "Alright, Sugar Mama!"

I couldn't wait to begin decorating. But now house rich and cash poor, we were just barely making ends meet, even with my promotions, bonus increases, and Miguel's intermittent work. So I made the curtains for our front windows because we couldn't afford the ones I really wanted, and we scoured garage and estate sales for our dresser, dining table, and TV stand. Any vacations we took were to visit family, and our infrequent dates were to industry restaurant openings where our meals would be comped. But we were happy, mostly.

Miguel had been auditioning and working odd jobs for nine months without a steady theater job when he got the call that a workshop of a show he had been a part of was moving forward. The musical was called *If/Then* and starred Broadway legend Idina Menzel, who was about to take over the lives of preschoolers everywhere as Elsa in *Frozen*. The production would start with a three-month run in Washington, DC, in the fall of 2013 before transferring to Broadway in the spring of 2014.

While we were grateful for the additional income, it came at a cost. I took a 7 AM train into the city so I could get in eight hours at the office before rushing back to New Jersey to pick up a nearly two-year-old Jackson from his day care before 6 PM. My train home literally passed Miguel's as he headed into the city for his show. After getting Jackson dinner and putting him to bed, I would open my laptop and work until midnight, making sure the evening's events had gone smoothly and prepping for the following day. Miguel would crawl into bed around one in the morning, and we would repeat it all the next day. Because Miguel had weekend performances as well, we only saw each other on Sunday mornings and Monday evenings.

Somehow, even though we were rarely home and awake at the same time, we managed to get pregnant: another boy. Naming Jackson had gone something like this:

"How about Jack? After my grandpa."

"Eh, I shared a cat with an ex named Jack. What about Jackson?"

"I like it."

"Jackson Miguel?"

"Done."

Coming up with a second boy name was proving more challenging. My dad refused to refer to the coming child as simply "the baby" and dubbed him Elvis in the interim.

"Why Elvis?" I asked him.

He replied, "The better question is, why *not* Elvis?"

Maybe it was because Jackson had unlocked my heart's capacity for maternal love or perhaps every pregnancy is different, but with Elvis I experienced a stronger prenatal connection. If Jackson had been trying to take over my body, Elvis felt more like a respectful roommate. By our twenty-week ultrasound I was starting to feel Elvis move, and he was so gentle, more like a butterfly than Jackson's battering ram.

Miguel and I settled into our usual positions for the scan. Me, on the table with my belly bare and slimed with goo, and Miguel in the chair next to me holding my hand. Photos of the technician's children lined her desk. She greeted us warmly and began her arduous task of taking all of Elvis's required anatomical measurements. We listened to his heartbeat. It seemed so strong for his being so small. And then the technician grew quiet. At first, I thought it was because she was so focused, so dedicated. But her comforting smile had been replaced with a furrowed brow and downturned lips. Miguel squeezed my hand, our eyes fixated on the black-and-white monitor before us, searching for clues in the shifting fuzzy masses.

"Is everything okay?" I finally got up the courage to ask.

"I'm not allowed to share any information. Your doctor will discuss the results with you."

The entire scan took nearly an hour. After I cleaned up, we were led to my doctor's office. Miguel and I sat in two cushioned chairs across from a large wooden desk and waited for the doctor to examine the results, or finish with another patient, or place her lunch order with the office manager—who knows.

By the time she entered, which could have been five or forty-five minutes later, I was already three tissues deep.

"There were a few measurements from the ultrasound that are concerning. I would like you to get a second opinion with the maternal-fetal specialist at the hospital," she said calmly.

"What does that mean? What are you seeing?" asked Miguel.

"I don't want to jump to conclusions without more information. At the hospital they have stronger equipment and can better advise you." There was sympathy in her voice, but her tone also made clear that we would not be getting anything else from her in that moment.

I called the hospital and was able to make an appointment for the following day. Then I took the train to work and pretended everything was okay because I didn't know what else to do.

ONE, TWO, THREE, *four, five . . . wait did I count that one already?*
For the second time in as many days, I was lying on a table, in another silent room, for another grueling scan. While the technician moved the wand over my swollen belly, I counted the square ceiling tiles, trying to hold in my fear-soaked sobs so that she could get the necessary pictures.

"Just a little bit longer, Mrs. Cervantes," the technician said.

Six, seven, eight. Tears momentarily blurred my vision. I'd lost my place on the ceiling. *One, two, three, four* . . .

Shortly afterward, the technician finished, and the doctor knocked on the door.

"Hi," she said, slowly entering the room. It was just one word, but her tone told us all we needed to know.

"Hi," Miguel replied for both of us, holding my hand and feigning strength.

She sat down in the chair the technician had been using moments before and placed a manila file, Elvis's file, on the counter next to her.

"Your baby has a condition called thanatophoric dysplasia. This condition causes several major health issues, but most concerningly, his rib cage is too small. As a result, his heart is taking up most of the space, resulting in severely underdeveloped lungs." While her words were harsh, her tone was not. "I am so sorry. There is no grey area here; this is one of the most severe fetal anomalies I have seen. You might be able to carry to term, but the condition will be fatal at birth. However you choose to proceed, we will support your decision. Again, I am so sorry."

We would learn that this condition, while genetic, was not hereditary and was as random and unlucky as a lightning strike. Also, that "thanatophoric" is Greek for "death-bearing." Before we left the hospital, a nurse gave us the names and numbers of two doctors whom we could call about terminating the pregnancy if that was the direction we chose. And then, tear-streaked and puffy-faced, I walked past the other pregnant women in the office, who didn't have the contact information for abortion providers in their pocket, and out to our car.

As terrible a decision as it was to make, it was not a difficult one. I thought of having clients, coworkers, and strangers comment on my growing belly, not knowing that the baby's birth would be his death. Of having to explain to Jackson that his brother, who he had watched grow in mommy's tummy, would not be coming home from the hospital.

And then of pushing through contractions only to hold my son as he suffocated—if he even survived that long.

No. We would not be doing any of that.

This decision was deeply personal, and it was ours to make. I do not now, nor have I ever, regretted it. Not when I felt him move for the last time, not when I was blinded by the pain of the induced contractions, and not when I woke up from the anesthesia and knew that he was gone.

The rest of the day following surgery, I thought I was going to be okay. I hated that we lost Elvis, but people lose pregnancies all the time. We would try again; we would be okay. And then the drugs wore off, and I woke up the next morning with an empty uterus. And I was not okay.

Then my milk came in, and I was not okay.

Then I ran into a friend from college who could have sworn they saw I was pregnant on Facebook. And I was really not okay.

My grief caught me off guard over and over again. I had thought because I never held him that the loss would somehow be easier to come to terms with. But I loved Elvis, I had felt him move inside me, he was real to me . . . but only me. Miguel grieved a dream, the idea of a child, but it wasn't the same for him as it was for me. He also didn't have postpartum hormones surging through his body.

For weeks, I forced space between us. I resented how much easier all of this was for Miguel. I *had* to tell anyone who had physically seen me since I began showing what had happened. Miguel didn't have to tell anyone he didn't want to. Then I had to worry about *what* to tell people. Did I choose to be vague and say, "We lost the pregnancy," and let them come to their own conclusions? Or did I give them the full story and risk their judgement?

"Hey, baby," Miguel said coming up behind me as I was picking out clothes for the day. He reached out to put his hand on my bare waist and I flinched. I hadn't meant to, but I couldn't help it. Physical touch, from Miguel specifically, made me think of sex, which made me think of being pregnant, and I couldn't go there. Sort of like when a bomb survivor ducks and covers when they hear fireworks. My body wanted to duck and cover from anything that might make a baby.

Even before I even turned to see Miguel's face, I knew my reaction had hurt him. But I didn't know how to make him understand without hurting him more.

"Wow," he said, a hostile tinge to his voice.

"I'm sorry. I'm just not ready to be touched like that yet," I tried to explain.

"Okay, but flinching away from me? Really? That sucked." He left me in our bedroom to get dressed alone.

For several more weeks, we tiptoed around each other, unable or unwilling to hold space for what the other was feeling. I wish I could say that we had some big talk that made it all better. But with time, as the hormones left my body, and I began acknowledging and processing my grief instead of wishing it would just go away, we fell back into usual patterns. Later, my mom would have a memorial stone carved that we placed in our yard, and I began collecting small Elvis mementos, a reminder that he had existed, if only within me. In the meantime, I so desperately wanted something else to focus on that I insisted we try for another baby as soon as I was medically cleared. Five months after saying goodbye to Elvis, the stick said pregnant again. A couple months after that, we learned it was a girl.

I HAVE ALWAYS known that I would name my first daughter Adelaide. When I was growing up, there hung in my parents' bathroom a black-and-white photo in a gold oval frame of my mother's grandmother Adelaide Lucy. She passed away when my grandma was a teenager. I don't know much about her except that she had two children before her husband passed away, and that during the Great Depression she found family for my great-uncle to live with, but she had to place my grandma in an orphanage in Harlem because the job she found as a live-in housekeeper wouldn't allow her to bring her daughter with her. Until she fell ill and passed away, Adelaide had visited my grandmother every weekend.

While her story is tragic, whenever I think of Adelaide, it is her strength I marvel at. It reminds me that even when we don't feel like we have a choice in a matter, we always do. Adelaide could have refused to part with her children and been forced into soup lines and tenements like so many during the Great Depression. All three of them could have died. But instead, she made the more difficult decision and sent her children into what she hoped would be a healthier and safer future. There is always a choice. Even if all the options are terrible, even if the answer seems obvious, the choice is still there to be made.

While I now had a newfound appreciation for the miraculousness of the birth of a healthy baby, I still found pregnancy as a whole unpleasant. Perhaps even more so now that I had a better understanding of how many ways a pregnancy could go wrong. That said, I thoroughly enjoyed nesting, specifically designing the nursery. Jackson's had a train theme, an ode to my dad's career at Union Pacific. Inspired by my trip to Tanzania, I had planned a safari-themed room for Elvis and already started collecting a few items, tucking them away in the closet until it was a socially acceptable time to decorate his room. That time never came for Elvis, but I decided that I still loved the theme and would hold on to the items for the next baby.

Some people have prophetic dreams. Dreams that give them direction or premonitions about what is to come. I do not believe that I have psychic talents; however, I have had two prophetic dreams in my life. One was that I was going to own a pair of yellow galoshes. Actually, that one may be closer to manifesting because shortly after the dream I just went and bought a pair, which I still own, adore, and wear whenever the sky is sad. The other prophetic dream I've had was that the baby in my belly was surrounded by ladybugs. In the dream, I called my baby "my Adelaideybug."

I called my mom to tell her as soon as I woke up from my dream. "Mom, you'll need to return anything you've already purchased for the safari nursery. Adelaide's nursery is going to have a ladybug theme." Within moments a shared Pinterest board had been created. Before I even held her, Adelaide had a ladybug rocking chair, Halloween costume, and wall decals.

Decorating a nursery that was exclusively Adelaide's allowed me to begin healing from Elvis's loss. It cemented something that in my heart I already knew: Adelaide was not replacing Elvis. She was not instead of; she was an addition.

The week before Adelaide's due date Mom flew up so she could be on hand for her birth.

"You know," Mom said, standing in Adelaide's nursery and admiring how it had all come together. "Ladybugs are a sign of good luck."

She hugged me, my lucky little Adelaideybug squished inside me and between us. Together we formed our own living nesting doll. I couldn't wait to meet her and hoped that I could always keep her just as safe as she was now, sheltered by two generations of love.

CHAPTER NINE
The Denialist

Adelaide came five days early, on October 17th, just as the leaves were beginning to brown.

"Was she born breach?" the postpartum nurse asked during Adelaide's initial exam.

She hadn't been. In fact, aside from her shoulder getting hung up, the labor and delivery had been surprisingly fast and simple compared to the hours of pushing and multiple interventions needed to bring Jackson into the world. When the nurse laid Adelaide in all her gooey glory on my bare chest, her dark grey-green eyes had locked onto mine within moments. She looked so much like her brother, sharing their father's eye shape and brow line—so much for Mig's Valentine's song about our child having my eyes.

"You see here? She's a little floppy and how her legs rest in a froggy position like this? That usually happens in breach babies," the nurse said, pulling me from my reverie. "Would you like her with you or in the bassinet?"

"With me," I answered curtly.

Instead of being concerned by her professional evaluation, I was filled with a defensive rage. How dare this nurse judge my hours-old baby (even if that was her professional job). All newborns are floppy (even if she holds dozens of newborns a day and has a much better gauge on these things than I do). Jackson had opened my heart to the joy, adoration, and frustration of motherhood. Then Elvis came along and left the door gaping open, leaving me exposed to all of motherhood's wild elements. Adelaide had followed up her brothers by taking the door off its hinges altogether. The love I felt for this small creature was so intense in its immediacy it was almost painful. As if I was now holding my very life force outside of my body.

Floppy frog legs aside, they let us take Adelaide home on time. Just as Jackson had done, Adelaide would sleep in a small bassinet next to our bed before moving into her own room several months later. Our first night at home, I awoke at 5 AM in a panic. Adelaide had never cried to feed as I had expected her to. I scanned her body for signs of life and watched with relief as her tiny chest rose and lowered with each breath. She was supposed to be eating every two or three hours. It had been almost seven.

I began to set alarms so neither of us would forget it was time for her to eat. But even then, at her one-week checkup, the pediatrician noted that Adelaide had lost much more than the typical 10 percent of her birth weight. Because I was breastfeeding, there was no way to know how much milk she was getting. So before and after each feeding, we laid her in a glass bowl on a small fruit scale, like an Anne Geddes calendar model, and recorded her weight.

I was concerned but not alarmed. I knew all babies developed differently. She just needed a bit more time to build up her strength, and she would be fine. Besides, we had already undergone our life-shattering tragedy. The doctors themselves had called Elvis's condition a genetic lightning strike. We knew that Adelaide did not have what

Elvis did, and the odds that a different kind of lightning could strike our family seemed infinitesimally low.

After a couple of weeks of closely monitoring her breastmilk intake, and at times using a medicinal dropper to feed her, Adelaide began to put on weight. I was so relieved when she narrowly avoided a "failure to thrive" diagnosis and readmittance to the hospital.

Mommy, tell me again about when I was a baby, and you had to weigh me in a bowl! I imagined Adelaide asking us when she was older.

Over the next few weeks, I did my best to avoid comparing Adelaide's newborn development with Jackson's. Besides, Adelaide *had* to be okay *because* Elvis wasn't.

When we arrived at the doctor's office for Adelaide's two-month checkup, a nurse handed me a piece of paper listing age-appropriate milestones:

- Holds head steady
- Bears weight on legs
- Tries to lift head and shoulders

There wasn't a single item I could confidently check off. How old had Jackson been when he'd hit these milestones? It had only been three years ago, but I was struggling to remember now.

Aside from having tubes placed in his ears due to frequent ear infections, Jackson's early years had been uneventful. Now, at three years old, he was a happy kid who was always on the move. He knew all the words to the *Paw Patrol* theme song and insisted on wearing a firefighter hat backward wherever we went. He was obsessed with his daddy and loved singing into his toy microphone in between improvised dance breaks. Sure there was the occasional tantrum, and meals were delivered in a drive-by fashion since getting him to sit still at the table was impossible, but he was a typical, happy, healthy toddler.

We left the doctor's office that day with a referral to see a neurologist.

"As a precaution," her pediatrician had said.

Cognitively, Adelaide seemed to be doing well. She tracked our movements across the room, smiled at us, and laughed when we blew raspberries on her belly. But when I returned to work after three months' leave and Adelaide joined her brother in day care, it was hard to deny her lagging physical development in comparison with the other babies her age.

IT WAS THE darkest, coldest days of winter before we could get Adelaide in to see a neurologist. The hospital's automatic sliding doors opened to a lobby with hallways jutting off in a compass rose of directions. Following signs, we pushed a bundled Adelaide in her stroller and wove our way through the hospital labyrinth to the neurology clinic.

Neither Miguel nor I had much experience with hospitals or specialists. Outside of maternal health, the last time we had been in a hospital was when Miguel's father had passed away the year after our wedding. It suddenly dawned on me how much we took our health for granted.

After checking in at the front desk, I searched the crowded waiting room to see where Miguel had settled with Adelaide. There were children in wheelchairs, others with obvious developmental disabilities, and still others that appeared typical as far as I could tell. My last regular contact with anyone that had a disability was in high school when I took an inclusive gym class with the special education students. It was the best gym class of my life: everyone was a winner, no one noticed how uncoordinated I was, and I've never seen high school students happier. But it was just one period of the day, and then I went on with my life, not stopping to think about what my disabled classmates' day looked like. Then again, at sixteen I didn't really consider anyone's life before or after they entered mine.

A mother wiping a bit of drool from her son's chin caught me watching her. I smiled at her, and quickly made my way across the room to join Miguel. Already, this medical confrontation was loosening the doubts and fears that I had successfully tied away with strings of rational thought.

After twenty anxiety-ridden minutes, a nurse in brightly colored scrubs took Adelaide's vitals and led us to an exam room where we anxiously awaited the doctor. Miguel and I silently scrolled our phones for distraction until, after a quick knock, a middle-aged woman with a round face and a warm smile entered the room.

"Hi, I'm Dr. Ellis, and you must be Adelaide," she said to Adelaide, who was resting in my arms. I found this intriguing, considering Adelaide was only four months old and unable to respond, but also somewhat comforting.

We provided Dr. Ellis with Adelaide's brief medical history, and then she directed me to lay Adelaide on the paper-lined medical table. She examined her body from head to toe, looked into her eyes with a light, and used the mallet-looking thing that comes with every Fisher-Price doctor kit to check Adelaide's reflexes. It took several attempts and a lot of me willing Adelaide's little leg to kick before it finally moved ever so slightly. With Adelaide lying on her back, Dr. Ellis pulled her up by her arms just a few inches. Adelaide's head hung behind her. Then she lowered her back on the table before placing her in my waiting arms.

"Thank you, Adelaide," Dr. Ellis said before sitting in a rolling chair across from a computer monitor. "Her muscles are definitely hypotonic."

"What does that mean?" Miguel asked. After placing Adelaide in her stroller, I was starting to take frantic notes that I anticipated would fuel Google searches well into the night.

"Hypotonia means that she has low muscle tone. It doesn't mean that her muscles are weak, but at baseline, they are not holding tension. This is in contrast to someone who has hypertonic or stiff muscles, such as those with cerebral palsy. We can run a few tests to see if we can figure out why this is happening, but in most cases babies outgrow it."

"Outgrowing is good," I said, looking at Miguel for reassurance.

"However, she'll still require early intervention therapy services, and I'll get a few initial tests ordered to make sure there isn't something else we can diagnose that is treatable."

Treatable? As in there could be something going on that isn't treatable? I filed the thought away and nodded in agreement to her plan.

I wanted to hold on to the hope that this was something Adelaide would outgrow with time and some physical and occupational therapy. But sitting in the clinic waiting room, I'd been forced to face an alternative future. And yet test after test came back normal, clear, or negative, and at home, Adelaide was making slow but steady progress in her therapies. However, despite her progress, the gap was widening between her and her peers. I started to hope that maybe a test or two would come back with one of those treatable diagnoses that Dr. Ellis had mentioned.

My favorite day of the year had come and gone, and I was too distracted to notice. It was now May, and with no clear answers, the next test on the list was an electroencephalogram, or EEG. Dr. Ellis explained that she was fairly certain this test would also come back normal, but due diligence was required.

During this period of so much uncertainty, I was grateful for the significant distraction that work provided. Spring was our busiest season, and I was also secretly interviewing on the side. It had become clear that there was limited room for advancement, and I would need a company change to keep climbing.

Meanwhile, Miguel's last Broadway show, *If/Then*, had closed the previous spring. He had participated in a few workshops of new musicals and booked some TV work, but most of the time he was home—which currently suited our family well. To satisfy his inner Energizer Bunny, he had started a company teaching baseball to four- to six-year-olds, and a couple of times a week he led music classes for babies. I didn't know how Miguel did it. How he sat across from mothers or nannies with their healthy babies, listening to them complain about Isaac not sleeping through the night or celebrating Emma's new word while he smiled and crooned about fire trucks and taxicabs, knowing our seven-month-old daughter was struggling to meet even the most basic milestones.

"WEATHER PERMITTING, WE could host your cocktail hour on the patio overlooking the river. We would set up multiple bars, have servers pass canapés, and include several food stations. Shall we step outside so you can see it for yourselves?" I was giving a newly engaged couple a tour of the restaurant when my cell phone buzzed in my pocket. Miguel's name flashed on the screen. I excused myself to answer the call.

"Hey, I'm in the middle of a site visit. Can I call you back?" I asked.

"I think Adelaide just had a seizure."

My chest tightened. Adrenaline flooded my system.

"What happened? Is she okay?"

"She seems okay . . . yeah. I put her in the infant carrier to leave day care and half her face went limp." I could barely process what he was saying. There was indistinct chatter in the background punctuated with intermittent baby cries. He was still at the day care.

"What do I do? Do I take her to the pediatrician? Call 911?" He was speaking fast now, even for him. I imagined the women who ran the day care huddled around him and Adelaide.

"I—I don't know. How long did it last?" Maybe if I had more information, I would know what to tell him.

"A couple minutes? I'm not sure, it was over before Maria could call 911."

"But her face is fine now? She's fine?" My tone rose with each question I asked.

"She looks completely normal, as if nothing happened."

I found a colleague to take over my site visit and began contemplating the fastest way to get home: Taxi? Train? Swimming? In time,

I would learn the necessity of pre-calculating the fastest way back to Adelaide's side, but in that moment, the logistics of my routine commute were paralyzing. I had been so certain that she would be okay. We had lost Elvis. That was our life-defining asteroid.

The next few days ran together as the landscape around me became pocked and cratered.

I cried at my desk when Miguel sent me a picture of Adelaide at home, her head wrapped in gauze to cover the EEG electrodes that had been glued to her scalp. A ponytail of wires coming out the back connected to a small backpack by her side.

My body went cold when I stepped away from the dinner table to take a call from Dr. Ellis, letting me know the results of Adelaide's EEG were irregular. She wanted to admit Adelaide to the hospital the next day.

I clung to Miguel in the hospital hallway when the nurses wheeled Adelaide away for a lumbar puncture. Which was only moments before he had to leave us to go to the city for the biggest audition of his life.

Asteroids, I learned, are not fairly rationed.

CHAPTER TEN
The Passenger

The wildest thing about asteroids is that for all their power and devastation, they can't stop time. Life finds a way forward, and we are forced to keep up. But I wasn't thinking about asteroids when I looked down at my phone and saw the missed calls from Miguel.

Shit! I must not be getting service in here.

"I'll be right back," I told my friends and, as of that night, former colleagues, as I stood from the restaurant table. After five years, I was leaving Tom Colicchio's restaurant group, having worked my way up from an event coordinator to a senior sales manager, growing and overseeing a multimillion-dollar events department.

Whether I was working with celebrity chefs, UN delegations, or high-end event planners, each day had brought new menu challenges, sales goals, and personalities to manage. It was exciting and draining and entirely too stressful for a job I now understood was about enjoyment and celebrations, not life or death.

Although it was rewarding, it was not my passion. I wasn't a foodie in the way my colleagues were. Sure, I'd enjoy a delicious meal as much as the next person, but the food fads, the up-and-coming chefs, and the new restaurant openings that all my colleagues kept up with and the various industry blogs they subscribed to could barely hold my attention.

To keep up appearances, I successfully modeled a fake-it-till-you-make-it facade. I knew enough of the industry buzzwords to pass under the nose of even the most discerning chef de cuisine or general manager. I learned on the job by hanging out in the kitchen, studying what different ingredients looked like, attending the wine tastings the sommelier held for staff, and allowing Google to be my BFF: best food friend. At the end of the day, I hadn't been offered this job for my food and wine acumen but because I was Midwest nice, organized, and an overachiever.

Working in restaurants may not have been my dream, but I'd built a career out of it. A successful career that supported my family and gave me a purpose from which I derived significant value. I had put in the sixty-plus hour weeks, worked the holidays, and taken the panic-stricken calls from our clients at 11 PM, and it had paid off. I was all set to start a director-level position at a growing restaurant group the following Tuesday.

As I stepped out of the mood-lit restaurant and into an unusually hot and sticky May night, I selected Miguel's name from the Favorites list on my phone.

"Where have you been?" Miguel asked on the first ring.

"I'm so sorry! I didn't realize there was no cell service at the restaurant. Is Adelaide okay?" *For how long would our conversations need to begin with an Adelaide status update?*

"She's fine." He paused. "I got the job."

"Oh my god! Oh my god! Mig! Congratulations! Wait, which one: Broadway or Chicago?"

"Well, both."

Hamilton. Even if you've never seen a musical outside of that endearing production of *Annie* that your high school put on all those years ago, you've heard of *Hamilton: An American Musical.* This was May 2016, before the Tony Awards, the national tours, and Disney Plus. Kids weren't yet cosplaying the Schuyler sisters or our founding fathers. But Broadway-obsessed folks wouldn't shut up about it.

There had been several rounds of auditions, including the one that forced Miguel to leave Adelaide and me at the hospital as she was being steered away for a spinal tap. Despite the multiple callbacks, we had been careful not to get our hopes up. Miguel had gone in for Frankie Valli in *Jersey Boys* more times than I could count, often making it to the final round, but had never booked the job. He had even auditioned for *Hamilton* the previous year when they were preparing to transfer from The Public Theater to Broadway, but had never heard back.

This time, however, he had gotten *the* call. He had been offered the role of Alexander Hamilton's understudy for one month on Broadway. Then he would start rehearsals with the Chicago company, the first production outside of New York City, and open the show in Chicago that fall as Hamilton himself. This was big. Lottery-winning kind of big. If, you know, winning the lottery required decades of training, dedication, and talent, in addition to being the right person in the right place at the right time.

And all we had to do was pick up our family of four, leave behind the lives we had built for the last eleven years, including my career that had supported us for the last five of those years, and move halfway across the country to Chicago—in just twelve weeks.

The streetlights were suddenly blinding.

I JUMPED OUT of the yellow cab and ran toward the tunneled entrance to Penn Station. I just needed to make my train. A quick glance at the departure monitors told me I had four minutes before the 9:32 PM train left the station. Plenty of time. At this hour, the rush-hour herd to which I was accustomed had thinned out, allowing me to maintain a brisk hustle down to the train platform. I collapsed in an empty row with a full minute to spare.

In an attempt to still my elevated heart rate, I took a few deep breaths. Which might have worked had my heart been pounding due to my jaunt through the off-colored halls of New York's finest mass transit hall and not Miguel's life-altering phone call.

Several rows ahead of me, a man was folding his suit jacket into a pillow for a nap. The woman in front of him had her laptop resting on her pencil skirt, analyzing spreadsheets, with her heels subbed out for more sensible sneakers. Behind me, I could smell someone's McDonald's and hear muffled electronic music blasting through headphones. None of these people appeared to have just experienced a tectonic shift in their lives. For my fellow commuters, it was a typical Thursday night. I, on the other hand, thought I might puke.

I wanted to be unequivocally thrilled for Miguel, for our family. The role of Hamilton not only came with professional notoriety but also a major pay raise. I didn't know how much money you made from playing Hamilton, but I was going to guess that it was substantially more than playing guitar while singing a song about taking a taxi around New York City to an un-potty-trained audience.

A part of me was so freaking proud I wanted to wake the napping businessman in front of me to tell him the news, but as the train barreled forward, so did my understanding of the cosmic ripple effect at play: The day Miguel was scheduled to begin rehearsals here in New York was also supposed to be the start date of my new job. From there, Miguel had six weeks to rehearse before his first performance on Broadway, and then six weeks after that our family would move to Chicago.

Outside, the train tunnel's intermittent safety lights gave way to traffic lights and muted stars over eastern New Jersey. How fine the line is between stars aligning and stars colliding.

Had it really only been a week since Adelaide's seizure and two days since she'd been discharged from the hospital? Between my job transition and Miguel's auditions, I hadn't had the chance to process everything we'd learned during Adelaide's admission or the one conversation in particular that kept playing on a loop in my mind.

"We haven't been able to capture any seizures on Adelaide's EEG, but we are seeing epileptiform activity. This means she could have a seizure at any moment and confirms that what you saw at her day care was probably a seizure." Dr. Ellis was standing next to Adelaide's hospital crib, examining her just as she had done the first time we met. She finished her exam and looked up at Miguel and me.

"Adelaide has epilepsy."

Was this why she had such low muscle tone? Would she have more seizures? Could she be cured? Dr. Ellis hadn't been able to definitively answer any of our questions. But how could she not know? How was it possible that modern medicine didn't have answers? We'd been sent home with more questions than answers, along with a script for an anti-seizure medication that Dr. Ellis "hoped" would be effective.

"Now arriving at Mountain Station. Next stop, South Orange." The intercom announced as the train began to slow.

Spreadsheet lady had gathered her bags and was exiting the train. For a moment, I allowed myself to be caught in the tentacles of self-pity, imagining her return to her happy family, in her uneventful home, with her healthy children. She could have been distracting herself with work to disassociate from her own life's challenges, but I would never know.

Finally, my brain caught up with my more intuitive and roiling stomach: I would not be starting my new job.

There was no way I could have known all of this would happen when I accepted the position. But that did little to resolve the guilt settling over me or the looming dread for the phone call I had to make to my would-have-been boss. And then, just as quickly as the guilt rolled in, I could taste it shifting toward something closer to resentment. But resentment at what? Toward whom? Miguel? For booking the role of a lifetime? For likely improving the trajectory of our lives at the expense of my career and self-worth?

And there it was.

Rationally I knew this response was emotional and selfish, but fuck! I had already given up an acting career, now I was going to be expected to give up another?

"Now arriving at South Orange. Next stop, Maplewood."

I looked around the train. My napping friend was gone, and I could no longer hear the drum of an EDM beat behind me. I pulled my bags together, heavy with mementos that had adorned my desk only that morning.

The train doors opened in front of me. I stepped off the train onto the familiar platform with its charming German-style station house, now closed for the night. I had taken this train to and from work nearly every weekday for the last three years, and now I didn't know when I would take it again. When I would be in New York City again. When I would work again.

I had thrived on the perception of control—something I naively believed I held. Even after this illusion had been shattered time and again by a dominating boyfriend, an abusive director, or a fatal fetal anomaly. I had always been able to put the pieces back together, to build a new protective layer around myself. Convinced I had learned a lesson, that now I knew better, that this time would be different, only to have it torn aside yet again, like the curtain hiding the Wizard of Oz.

That morning, I had boarded the commuter train as a senior events manager in charge of a multimillion-dollar department. I had been Miguel's "sugar mama" and an all-powerful wizard responsible for my family's financial future and well-being. But walking home in the breezeless night, lit by garish streetlights and stripped of my titles, I was just Kelly.

IN THE WEEKS that followed, I felt like a passenger in my own life. I was aboard the train and it was moving full steam ahead, but I was on someone else's track. Someone else was conducting. In the past, when I felt I had lost control of my life, I had compensated by controlling what I ate. The temptation was there, but this time I chose to find control in Adelaide's care.

"Miguel, where have you been keeping all of Adelaide's medical records?" With our roles reversed and Miguel now working full-time, I was taking over as Adelaide's medical point person.

"Her records?"

"The papers they give you after each doctor appointment? With their notes and test results?"

"Ummm . . . on my desk? I think?"

Sure enough, Adelaide's medical records were on Miguel's desk—scattered all over his desk and in no particular order. Thankfully, opposites attract, and I *live* for a good reason to use a hole punch. Within hours, I had a binder filled with every test result, therapy report, and aftercare summary. I may not have been able to control much in my life, but I could still arm myself with data and details.

Meanwhile, Miguel had roughly six weeks to learn Alexander Hamilton's staging, emotional arc, and over nine hundred lines, including nearly thirty songs. I had never seen him so singularly focused. When he wasn't in the rehearsal studio working long hours with director Tommy Kail, music director Alex Lacamoire, or choreographer Andy Blankenbuehler (the trio lovingly referred to by fans as "The Cabinet"), Miguel was moving through the motions of home life with ear buds in place, listening to the soundtrack on repeat.

His first performance as Alexander Hamilton occurred at the matinee on Wednesday, July 13, 2016. I attended with my mother because Miguel's mom, Mary, was too nervous to watch his first performance. Which worked out well because we needed someone to watch the kids while I went to Chicago the following week to look for an apartment.

As my mom and I walked up to the theater, police were working to clear the streets of the hundred or so fans that had flooded the area in hopes of scoring lottery tickets to the sold-out show. That some of these people would be seeing my husband in the lead role was surreal. My hands started to shake, and I couldn't stop talking. It wasn't that I thought he would mess up, or if he did, that I would even be able to notice—but that I had never seen him take on a role of this magnitude before.

We were already settled into our front-row mezzanine seats when my phone dinged with a message from Miguel. It was a mirror selfie of him smiling in his costume. I was a little taken aback at how good he looked in his revolutionary wig with a ponytail.

"Let me see!" Mom said looking over my shoulder. I handed her my phone, thinking she would comment on how she thought he did or didn't look nervous. "Wow, and you get to have sex with him! Do they let you bring the costume home?"

I snatched my phone back from her quickly. Apparently, Mom's uptight demeanor had been relaxed by her recent retirement from her therapy practice.

Break a leg! I love you! I texted back as Mom proudly told the woman sitting next to her that her son-in-law would be starring in today's performance. I looked at the picture again. He did look really cute.

Dun duh-duh-duh-dun dun dun. The famous first notes resonated through the packed house. I had only seen *Hamilton* once before, the previous September after Miguel had surprised me with tickets for our anniversary. I had squeezed into the narrow seats at the Richard Rodgers Theatre eight months pregnant with Adelaide and, like most people, had been blown away by the show.

"My name is Alexander Hamilton . . ."

There he was, onstage, my husband. I might have squealed.

Miguel's performance was outstanding. Mom was in tears and speechless, the latter highly uncommon for her. Any nerves I had were long gone, replaced with the unencumbered excitement I had longed to feel when I had first learned that he'd landed this role. For a moment, my resentment abated, and I was just really freaking proud.

DAYS LATER, WITH Mary settled in with the kids, I boarded a plane to Chicago. I had four days to find a home for our family and a preschool for Jackson. There wouldn't be time to make a second trip, so I needed to make the most of this one. I asked my friend and old coworker, Marc, to join me in hopes of exploring the city and enjoying some much-needed downtime in between viewings.

Marc's dry humor had gotten me through many trying guests, and now I hoped it would provide some respite on this trip as well. Especially since the last time I had been to Chicago was to attend a Dave Matthews Band concert at Soldier Field when I was eighteen. Suffice it to say that, aside from a few well-known landmarks and the pizza style of choice, I knew almost nothing about the city.

Our first day in Chicago, we toured neighborhoods and a few homes with our realtors to get an idea of what I liked. Then after a late dinner, we crashed at our Airbnb in Wrigleyville. The next morning, I was getting ready to look at more apartments when Miguel called.

"Hey, so Adelaide keeps doing these weird head drops. Mom and I thought it was just her bad head control, but she keeps doing it." As dramatic as his chosen profession was, Miguel was not one to alarm easily. If he was bringing it up at all, then he was concerned.

"Do you think it's a seizure?" I asked.

"It's different from the other one, but maybe? Should I call Dr. Ellis?"

I tried to stay calm, to think clearly. There was nothing I could do from Chicago. "Yes, but if you don't get a quick response and it keeps happening, I think you have to take her to the ER."

"Yeah. Okay, I'll keep you updated. Love you."

"Love you too." I stared out the window at the Chicago alley below. Why did I always have to be so far away when Adelaide needed me? I wanted to jump on the next plane to New Jersey. But I also needed to make sure our family had a home to move into in six weeks.

Throughout the day, Miguel updated me via text:

Spoke to Dr. Ellis. She wants to wait and see if it keeps happening. I'm supposed to call her back in a couple hours.

It's still happening. Left a message for Dr. Ellis.

Dr. said to bring her to the ER.

In the ER. They just paged a neurologist.

They're admitting her.

We're in a room and they're hooking her up to the EEG.

I tried to call Miguel a couple times, but each time he texted back that he'd call me when he could. Finally, as Marc and I were walking back into our rental to freshen up before dinner, Miguel called.

"What is going on? Is Adelaide okay?" I asked. The composure I had worked so hard to keep all day was popping off one overstretched button at a time. I sat down on my unmade bed.

"She's still doing the head drop thing a couple times an hour. It's getting worse. Actually, babe, one of the doctors is here to talk to us. I'm going to put you on speaker phone." Miguel sounded tired and anxious.

"Hi, I'm Dr. Aldaya, I work with Dr. Ellis and am the neurologist on service." She spoke with an air of authority, dry and to the point. "On Adelaide's EEG, we are seeing a brain wave pattern called hypsar-rhythmia, which is only seen in a form of epilepsy known as infantile spasms. Infantile spasms are incredibly serious and if left untreated can damage her brain. I am recommending we get her started on a medicine called Acthar immediately. It is a powerful medicine that is injected into her thigh and will hopefully stop the spasms. The side effects are intense, so she will need to stay inpatient while we monitor how she handles the drug and if it is working." The phone was shaking against my face. It took me a moment to realize that it was my hand shaking, not the phone.

I tried to picture the hospital room that I so badly needed to see—to be present in. I imagined Adelaide in the hospital crib, her head wrapped in gauze, and the doctor and Miguel on either side of her. "Acthar will cause her body to secrete extra steroids, so she will put on a lot of weight and get very puffy, lethargic, and irritable," the doctor continued. "It will significantly lower her immune response, and she could develop stomach ulcers. We will be testing her blood pressure and stools daily to be sure she is tolerating the medication. All that said, it is the best medication we have to treat infantile spasms."

"How long will she need to stay in the hospital?" I finally found my voice as Marc came quietly into the bedroom and sat down on the bed next to me. He didn't say a word, he just started rubbing my back.

"It depends on how well she responds to the medicine. A week at least, probably longer. Once the paperwork is signed, we will send off for the medication. We should have it in the hospital by tomorrow or the next day."

"Why can't she start it tonight?" I couldn't believe I was advocating for my daughter to be injected with a terrifying medicine *sooner*.

"Acthar is very expensive and not used often enough to be kept in the hospital's pharmacy. We will do everything we can to get it here as soon as possible. Now, if it's okay, I'd like to examine Adelaide." I heard footsteps and some rustling. Miguel took me off speaker phone.

"You there?" He sounded deceptively closer.

"I'll start looking at flights as soon as we're off the phone," I answered.

"Did you find an apartment?"

"I put an offer on one, but we were outbid. We're supposed to see a place tomorrow that looks promising, but I should be at the hospital with you."

"I know you want to come home. I want you to come home. But we need a place to live. Mom is here, we can figure this out for two days until you get back. She's not starting this medication until tomorrow at the earliest anyway." I knew he was right, but how could I stay in Chicago when my world was falling apart in New Jersey? "I gotta go, the doctor has more questions. I love you."

I kept the phone up to my ear for several seconds after the line went silent. Body-shaking sobs erupted from my chest. I collapsed into Marc's shoulder and stayed there for quite some time. I hated that this was happening, I hated not being there, I hated feeling like we were on a runaway train and there was no way to stop or even steer it.

"At least you know Miguel is super organized and will be able to remember everything the doctors say," Marc offered sarcastically. I snorted a disgusting mix of tears and snot, reinforcing that I'd brought along the correct friend.

The following afternoon, from the airport, I digitally signed a rental agreement on an apartment I'd viewed hours earlier. Within minutes of landing in Newark, I was in a cab, weaving through traffic on I-78 and headed to the hospital. None of this felt real. It was too dramatic to be real, as if I was playing a role in a movie and any minute a director would yell "cut" and we would have to take it again from the top. What I wouldn't have given to get my hands on that script.

The sun had long since set by the time I walked into Adelaide's dimly lit hospital room. Mary sat with Adelaide in a chair by the window as a nurse prepared medications on a tray in the corner.

"Adelaide, there is someone very special here to see you!" Mary whispered.

"Hello, my sweet girl! I missed you so much!" I cooed. Adelaide didn't respond to my voice. She didn't look my way and her face didn't brighten. She just laid there, in her Nana's arms, not moving.

"Her nurse was just about to give her another dose of the fancy new medicine. Why don't you hold her?" Mary handed me Adelaide, which, given all the cords from the EEG, was a logistical challenge. The little girl I now held in my arms was a shadow of the one I had left just a few days earlier. Moments later, when the nurse administered the steroid-inducing shot in her thigh, Adelaide didn't utter a sound.

CHAPTER ELEVEN
The Support Staff

Adelaide was hospitalized for a total of four weeks as we tried to gain control of the infantile spasms. By the time we were discharged, less than two weeks before our moving day, she had regressed to the developmental stage of a newborn.

The doctors had warned me not to google infantile spasms, that if I had questions to ask them. Which was ridiculous advice; of course I was going to google it. Opening my laptop, I hoped to discover that the spasms were curable, that Adelaide would go on to lead a typical life. Searching website after website, I found some cases where that was true, but it was significantly less likely to happen if the child had any developmental delays or additional symptoms prior to the spasms. In those instances, the child often experienced significant disabilities and, in some cases, premature death.

That wasn't going to happen to Adelaide. I wouldn't let it.

I resisted the temptation to slam my laptop shut and instead committed to learning everything I could about her various symptoms and test results. With no medical background and having received my lowest grade ever in human physiology, I was light-years outside of my comfort zone. But that no longer mattered because my daughter was sick, and I needed to know I was doing everything possible to help her.

When I wasn't attempting to read through scientific white papers with a medical dictionary open in a browser to the side, I was researching doctors in Chicago, making appointments, getting quotes from moving companies, and doing everything else that is necessary to move a family of four halfway across the country. And all from Adelaide's hospital bedside, which I only left every few days to return home to see Jackson and shower.

Once she was discharged, the remaining weeks before the move were a mad dash to prepare for our time away. Miguel's contract was for twelve months, and because he had never been in a show for longer than a year, I assumed we would be moving back home when the contract was up. I sorted through what could be left behind in storage and what was coming with us, being sure to pack a few of Jackson's old toys in a trunk from Miguel's *Spelling Bee* touring days to take with us for when Adelaide recovered. But for the first time in five years, I was having trouble imagining our future. Everything about our current state felt temporary—or maybe I needed it to be temporary. We were temporarily moving to Chicago, I was temporarily not working, and Adelaide's development was temporarily delayed.

WHAT TURNED OUT to be the most temporary was our time away from the hospital. Within four days of arriving in Chicago, Adelaide was admitted once again, this time via ambulance. Adelaide had been inconsolable that morning—nothing would calm her. Perhaps to be safe, or maybe out of desperation, I'd taken her to the pediatrician, who after triple-checking Adelaide's alarmingly low blood oxygen levels had in turn called the paramedics.

At the hospital, we would discover that Adelaide's low muscle tone was causing her to aspirate her formula, and she had developed pneumonia. To prevent further infection, the doctor ordered a nasogastric tube, or NG tube, to be used for all liquid and medicine intake moving forward. Thankfully, oxygen cannulas and medical tubing no longer reminded me of the doom they portended on 1980s soap operas, though I certainly wasn't prepared for the crash course in nursing that accompanied them.

"It's time to change out Adelaide's tubing. You ready to give it a try?" the nurse asked me. Over the last two days, I had watched the nurses thread the thin NG tube up Adelaide's nose, down her esophagus, and into her stomach. But I was not a nurse, and the whole thing made my stomach turn.

"I'd rather watch you do it again, if that's okay," I answered, getting up from the pull-out chair by the window that doubled as my bed.

"The doctors won't allow you to be discharged until you can do it on your own. You can do it," she said encouragingly, before adding, "You have to."

Damn it.

I walked slowly to the sink next to Adelaide's bed and washed my hands. When I turned back to her bed, the nurse had the metal tray prepped with everything I would need: the tube, a single-use packet of lubricating jelly, medical tape, scissors, and a syringe.

"Hey, Adelaidey, we're going to do this together, okay?" At the sound of my voice Adelaide stopped sucking her thumb and looked at me inquisitively with her big hazel eyes.

"I'll hold her head still so she doesn't move around too much for you," the nurse offered, placing her hands gently on either side of Adelaide's head. "First, you need to measure how much tubing you need by holding it up outside her nose and estimating the length to her stomach." I did as the nurse instructed. "Good, now cut off the extra. Okay, put a little bit of that lubricating jelly on the small end. And now you can thread it up her nostril, and it should go fairly easily down her throat."

Deep breaths. You can do this. You have to do this.

Adelaide squirmed as I felt the tube work its way up her nose. The turn down her throat was not as easy.

"Wiggle it a bit, and push again gently."

I tried again. This time the tube moved down her throat.

"You did it! Not so bad, right?" The nurse was smiling at me.

I felt like I was going to pass out. Only when I exhaled did I realize it was because I'd been holding my breath.

"Now all you have to do is stick the syringe in the port end here and pull back to make sure you get a little gastric acid. That way you know the tube didn't drop into her lungs, which would be bad—you don't want to be sending liquid into her lungs. Then tape the extra tubing to her cheek, and you're good to go!"

I stared at her blankly before repeating back, "Lungs bad, stomach good. Got it." I did not, in fact, feel like I "had it." Or had anything close to resembling "it."

With the tubing in place, Adelaide went right back to sucking her thumb, completely unbothered by her new accessory. The doctor had explained that Adelaide would need this tube until her swallow reflex got stronger or until we elected for a gastronomy tube—aka G-tube—which bypassed her nose and throat by surgically placing a direct port to her stomach near her belly button. She wasn't going to need that, though, I decided. We would do all the feeding therapy she required and get her strong enough so she could swallow again. This too could be temporary.

While I was learning basic medical procedures, Miguel was responding to a frenzy of interview and appearance requests on top of his already intense rehearsal schedule. One of those requests involved the opportunity to throw out the first pitch at a Chicago Cubs baseball game at the famed Wrigley Field—just one day before Adelaide was scheduled to be discharged from the hospital.

"Wait, your husband is throwing the first pitch at the game today, and you're not going?" asked Katie, the nurse assistant who had been helping care for Adelaide the last few days. She was in her early twenties with dark hair and kind eyes, and she almost always had a smile on her face—except for right now, as she stared at me in disbelief.

"I've never left Adelaide alone in the hospital before," I admitted.

"What? You don't trust me?" Her smile was back. "I'll get you the phone number to the front desk, and you can check on her as many times as you want. But you're going to that game." Katie had been a light to me the last few days as I'd vented about my anxiety around Adelaide's NG tube, being new to Chicago, and navigating this wild life without much local support. She'd even offered to babysit Jackson and Adelaide whenever Miguel and I had date nights or events to attend. It made me consider venting my frustrations to strangers more often.

From Wrigley Field's third baseline, with the sun high in the sky and a slight breeze in the air, Jackson and I listened as they announced Miguel's name over the loudspeakers. I tried to take in the crowd, the dirt beneath my sneakers, and the famous ivy-covered walls. Dad had brought Cam and me to see a game here once when we were kids. He'd told us it was one of the best stadiums in the country for watching a ball game. I wished Dad could be with us now. I wished I could go back to being a kid and listen to Dad talk about baseball as he detangled my hair. I wished my greatest concern was still finding the just right crayon color.

The sold-out crowd of over forty-one thousand people cheered as Miguel's name was announced and he walked up to the pitcher's mound. His throw was high and outside, but masterfully handled by the catcher. Then he signed autographs, and we stood for pictures as a family—minus one. Looking around the stadium, I marveled at how all of this could be happening while our daughter lay alone in a hospital crib with a tube up her nose—and no one here knew.

In an interview not long after that game, Miguel would describe our concurrent journeys with *Hamilton* and Adelaide as being like holding onto a rocket in one hand while dragging a parachute behind us in the other. The highest of highs coexisting with the lowest of lows—it was quickly becoming a reoccurring theme in our lives.

IN KEEPING WITH our new life theme, just two days before *Hamilton* Chicago's opening night was Adelaide's first birthday. Despite everything going on, the event planner in me never even considered not throwing her a party. So with our home decked out in pink and gold balloons, streamers, and linens, we invited all four of the Chicagoans we knew to join us, along with our family members who were in town for the *Hamilton* opening, for a small birthday celebration.

Just before our move to Chicago, the medications had finally succeeded in stopping the infantile spasms. Unfortunately, a new seizure type had taken their place. In an attempt to gain control of these new seizures, we'd started Adelaide on a medical ketogenic diet: high fat, very low sugar. There would be no cake smash, no pictures of a frosting-covered baby. We couldn't even give her the smallest taste of her cake for fear of throwing her body out of ketosis. But that didn't mean she couldn't still look adorable in a white onesie with a pink and gold tutu and headband.

When our guests had departed and our home had been restored to its pre-party state, I retreated toward our bedroom to dispose of the fake smile I had expertly applied for the day's festivities. But the smile had been my armor, and without it I felt weak. My legs grew heavy as exhaustion set in. Unable to take another step, I crumpled to the floor near our bedroom door.

Holding my knees to my chest, I stared out our bedroom windows. From where I sat, all I could see was the overcast sky. This wasn't right. This wasn't how her first birthday was supposed to be. Everything felt forced and unstable, like when you are trying to repair something but your efforts feel like they're only making things worse.

Several minutes later, I heard Miguel coming up the stairs. He didn't say anything at first. He just joined me on the floor.

"Jackson took his first steps the night before his first birthday," I finally said.

"I remember," Miguel replied solemnly. "But we have no reason to believe that Adelaide won't walk someday too."

"She's one year old and can't roll over or sit. She's only just starting to be able to hold her head up again, and now there's a new kind of seizure we can't control. What is her future going to look like? Will she ever speak? Go to school?" The tears were coming hot and fast, and I choked on the questions as they came out of my mouth.

"Until someone can tell us definitively that Adelaide will not be able to do something, then the possibility is there. And we have to live within that cone of possibility. Right now, everything is still possible," Miguel answered.

While it felt irresponsible to pretend like Adelaide could still lead a typical life, in that moment all I wanted was for someone to tell me that it was all going to be okay. On the floor beside Miguel, I chose to lean into his hope. And he wasn't wrong: with only a collection of symptoms and no overarching diagnosis, no one could tell us otherwise. Miguel's cone of possibility was only a philosophical Band-Aid, but that and a glass of wine got me off the floor that evening.

Two nights later, with the kids safely in nurse assistant Katie's care, Miguel took the stage on opening night to an eruption of cheers and applause. The energy was more akin to a rock concert than a Broadway musical. It's possible, as Miguel's biggest fan, that I got caught up in the excitement of it all, cheering and hollering at each of his stage entrances, particularly at the end of the song "My Shot."

"Excuse me, you are infringing on my ability to enjoy the show," said the woman sitting in front of me.

My cheeks flushed with embarrassment at being singled out. I checked myself. Yes, I'd been loud. But then again, this was an opening night! Everyone was loud!

Even so, "I'm so sorry" was all I had the courage to say.

My sister-in-law offered to let her know who I was and that I could cheer as loud as I damn well pleased. I quietly thanked her for the offer but passed. As the show went on, though, my embarrassment was replaced with pride. That was *my* husband up there, and together we had kept our daughter alive for the last year! I had learned to give shots, take blood pressure, test urine and poop, *and* thread a tube up her nose down to her stomach (*stomach good, lungs bad*), all while Miguel learned the tens of thousands of words required to play this role. That night, we celebrated so much more than the opening of the show, and quite frankly, the woman sitting in front of me could fuck off. I would never have said that to her, but I thought it really hard.

WITH THE PRODUCTION now open, we stumbled along trying to find yet another new rhythm for our life. When Miguel was home, he was often resting his body, his voice, or both. He had never taken on such a physically demanding role, and it required him to condition not unlike a professional athlete. The responsibility he felt to his cast, the producers, and audience was immense—but was easily bested by the pressure he felt to provide financial stability for our family. Not least of which was our health insurance, which depended on the number of weeks a year Miguel was employed in a show.

I was walking out of the pharmacy with the latest anti-seizure medication Adelaide's doctor had prescribed when I caught my husband's face out of the corner of my eye. There he was, in black and white, right next to Lin-Manuel Miranda on the cover of *Chicago* magazine. The juxtaposition of my errand with his cover shot was not lost on me: just more rockets and parachutes. I shoved the prescription in my oversized mom bag and headed toward the parking lot. Miguel would need to leave for the theater soon.

By the time I got home, Miguel's car service was already waiting outside to whisk him away to the theater. I came in the back door and was greeted by Tabasco and then Miguel, who kissed me goodbye before heading toward the front door.

"Did Adelaide get her afternoon meds?" I yelled after him.

"Uh . . . no? I don't know what she's supposed to get."

"She's gotten the same medication at the same time of day for the last week. If you didn't know, why didn't you call me?" I knew the pressure Miguel was under was great, but while he was playing cover boy and receiving thunderous applause, I was left to manage every other detail of our lives.

"I didn't know. It's hard to keep track when her meds are always changing." He was defensive but not apologetic—which only made me angrier.

"She is *your* daughter too! Why aren't you more invested in her care?" I shot back.

"Because that is your job." He said it matter-of-factly and without malice, without anger. I stared back, speechless. "I love you. I have to go to work. Chacho, baby girl, I'll see you in the morning!"

"Love you, Daddy!" Jackson called from the floor where he was building a colorful Lego spaceship.

Miguel closed the door behind him.

I stood in our entryway, frozen in disbelief. We had always managed our home and children together. We supported each other's ambitions; we were a team. But even as my ego seethed, there was a part of me that knew there was truth to his words. Adelaide's care was getting more complicated, not less. Without a point person, we ran the risk of giving her a double dose of a medication or missing it altogether. Still, I hadn't asked for this job, and more importantly, I didn't want it. But I couldn't resign or quit, so instead I awoke each morning to a life I didn't recognize, one where I had been demoted from breadwinner to support staff.

"Mommy, I'm hungry," Jackson said, looking up from his creation.

Rage crying would have to wait. Adelaide still needed her medications, and dinner had to be served: chicken nuggets and mac 'n' cheese for Jackson, baby food mixed with butter for Adelaide, and a can of soup for me. I got both children bathed and put to bed before delivering Adelaide's night meds through her nose tube and setting up her overnight feeding pump.

I was already in bed when Miguel texted that he would be home late. Friends had come to see the show, and he was joining them for a drink. I didn't respond.

The past six months had moved so quickly there hadn't been time to process it all. I had never wanted to be a housewife. In fact, one of the (many) reasons I hadn't gotten back together with Ryan was I didn't want to give up my ambition to support his. And now here I was, ten years later, living the life I had tried to run from. Of course it was more complicated than that. If Adelaide wasn't sick then I would probably have found a job in Chicago. But she needed me, our family needed me, and how lucky were we that Miguel was making enough money that we could afford to have me stay home?

I understood all this implicitly, yet still, the disparity in the quality of our lives was blinding me to the positives. It was more than the accolades and applause that Miguel was receiving (though that alone would have been more than enough to put Omaha Kelly over the edge). He had the freedom to schedule appointments, go out for drinks, or meet up with someone for dinner. I had yet to meet a friend, let alone dare to make plans, as they would have to work around both Miguel's schedule and Adelaide's appointments. And that was not even to mention Jackson's school and activities!

Mother, homemaker, and caregiver can all be fulfilling job titles on their own. But they had never been enough on their own for me. In the same way that acting in commercials hadn't been enough for me. Perhaps that makes me selfish or simply ambitious—though I don't know many men who have been forced to grapple with this differentiation.

For the entirety of my adult life, I had tied my identity to my career. It was the easiest barometer in my ever-evolving pursuit of my special self. However, now, the only identities I could see were "Miguel's wife" and "Mom"—which were and are important pieces of my identity, and inside my home were the most special titles I could achieve. But they couldn't be all there was or ever would be. It also didn't help that whenever we were in the hospital or at therapy or a doctor's appointment my name was rarely used.

Are you Mom?

Mom, what is her baseline?

Mom, we ordered her a disability placard for your car. It should arrive in the mail in a couple weeks.

Wait. What? When did she go from developmentally delayed to disabled?

And that was the issue. I wasn't just managing a home with a one-year-old and a four-year-old. I wasn't just learning my way around a new city, a new hospital system, a new medical world. I wasn't just grieving our community and my career that we'd left behind in New York. I was also grieving the life I had envisioned for my daughter and our family. A life as healthy, able-bodied people who moved through the world and checked off the boxes.

But who could I even talk to about all of this? My husband was starring in the most popular show in the world. We were making more money than we ever had and were attending exciting events with fascinating people. Who did I think I was to be resentful and depressed? Our life was charmed. I should be grateful. I should be happy.

But I wasn't, and the "shoulds" only made the pain sharper.

At my mom's urging, I had finally made an appointment to talk to someone. Catherine seemed nice enough, but she was young, maybe thirty, and her plentiful energy led me to believe she probably didn't yet have children of her own.

"What are your goals for therapy?" she asked.

Adelaide slept in her stroller next to me as I mulled over the question.

"I don't know. I miss the independence and purpose of my previous life. But those aren't realistic goals given the circumstances. I miss living in a world where hard work pays off. Because no matter how much time and energy I put into Adelaide, her progress is so slow and unsteady. Also, I know it's selfish, but I miss feeling valued by more than a four-year-old, a one-year-old, and my husband, but how can anyone else depend on me when all my time is taken by family?" I wiped the tears from my face with an already soggy tissue.

"It seems like control is a central theme here," Catherine observed.

No shit. "Yeah, that's kind of my thing."

"What if instead of focusing on all the parts of your life that are out of your control, you look for things that you can control."

"Sure, but controlling what my family has for dinner doesn't exactly fill the same need." I checked the clock on her desk to see how much longer I had to sit there.

"I'm going to give you some homework. I want you to buy a new notebook or journal and at the end of each day record everything you accomplished that day. I think when you see how much you are already doing, even if it's not exactly what you want to be doing, it may help you get over this first hump."

"Okay, but I already know I do a lot in a day. It's just that I find very little of it fulfilling. I know that sounds harsh. I love my family, I really do; I just need something else too."

"Absolutely. I still want you to give yourself credit for everything you are doing right now, and also to spend less time focusing on what you can't control."

I didn't even have the energy to read a book before bed, let alone compile self-congratulatory lists. But I didn't say that.

"Got it."

While my sessions with Catherine were likely numbered, I knew she was right about shifting my focus toward what I could control. Resentment-laden lists, however, were not going to be the catalyst. I was resisting these life changes because I hadn't wanted nor chosen them—but to what end? Why couldn't I just let go? I had felt something similar to this before, when my relationship with Ryan was crumbling and when we lost Elvis.

And then it clicked. I wasn't just resisting change. I was grieving.

In labeling my response as grief I started to see my efforts at refocusing not as an attempt to take back control but to heal. Okay, maybe it was more like finding where I could exert control *while* healing. I hadn't chosen this new life, but I could choose how I prioritized my energy. I couldn't control Adelaide's health or the progress she made, but I could make sure she had the best care. I couldn't control my husband (despite my best efforts), but I could let him know what I needed.

Even though I was still furious with Miguel for saying Adelaide's medical care was my job, he wasn't entirely wrong. That didn't mean he couldn't help, it just meant that I had to delegate. Which would require us both to level up our communication: emotionally and logistically. Not an easy task for someone who saw asking for help as a weakness (me) and someone who was easily distracted (him).

OF COURSE, I wasn't the only family member who'd been forced onto a diverging path. Jackson had started a new preschool and was also navigating life with a sick sister. The difference was that when *he* looked at Adelaide, he didn't see all the things she "should" be doing. He had no expectations for her; she was just his baby sister, and he loved her. He "wrestled" with her, cuddled her too hard, and gave her smooshie kisses on her cheek. I desperately wanted to see her through his eyes, to accept her as she was.

Over the last few months, Adelaide's swallow reflex had not gotten stronger, and in another hit to my illusion of control, we had acquiesced to the more comfortable and convenient G-tube solution. Miguel might have been lost if I didn't tape Adelaide's medication list to the fridge, but he was typically a step ahead of me in accepting necessary interventions to maintain her quality of life.

"Cone of possibility: it's not that she won't ever swallow liquids again, she just needs more help right now," he'd tried to reassure me.

Even though I knew it was the right decision, a highly irrational part of me felt defeated, as if Adelaide needing the G-tube meant I had somehow failed her. As if I had given up on her. Thank goodness Jackson and Miguel saw it differently.

"Chacho, look!" Miguel said, pointing to the clear plastic G-tube port protruding from Adelaide's bare belly. "Adelaide doesn't need her nose tube anymore. Now she has an awesome new tummy checker."

"Cool! It's like she has *two* belly buttons!" Jackson exclaimed excitedly before trying to blow raspberries on the G-tube-free side of his sister's stomach. Adelaide paused sucking her thumb to look in Jackson's direction. Taking this as an encouraging sign, Jackson tried again, but instead of laughing, Adelaide swung and hit his head. Her motor control was still significantly delayed, making it hard to tell if the contact had been purposeful. However, her sigh of relief after Jackson jumped back left little doubt about her intent.

"She hit me!" he yelled.

Miguel and I stifled laughter. "Adelaide," I said, "That wasn't very nice." Adelaide just looked at me, her thumb back in her mouth. "Adelaide doesn't have words, so she uses her body and eyes to talk to us. I think she was telling you she didn't like that," I explained to Jackson.

"I just wanted to make her laugh . . ." Jackson mumbled, leaving the room with a pout.

Later that night, Jackson was watching TV before bed. Adelaide was sitting in her infant chair sucking her thumb and contently watching beside him. With both children safely occupied, I headed into the kitchen to clean up after dinner. And then I heard something.

Pfffft.

I turned off the water.

Grabbing a dish towel to dry my hands, I jogged out of the kitchen. I hadn't left the kids alone for more than three minutes, and Jackson knew better than to try and move his sister.

As I turned the corner, I heard it again, *Pfffft,* and then—*was that a child laughing or crying?* Our dining room table was blocking my view of the kids, so I sprinted the last few steps.

"*Mommy!* Watch this!" Jackson was grinning ear to ear. Adelaide's chair had been turned away from the TV and was now facing Jackson, who was walking toward an armchair.

"Oh, that was a nice long walk," Jackson said, feigning exhaustion. "I think I'll just have a seat in this comfy chair." He sat down.

PFFFFFffffffft.

The low flapping sound fluttered to a stop. Jackson had sat on a whoopee cushion, and Adelaide was now unabashedly giggling in response.

"She's laughing, Mommy! She thinks it's funny!"

I was so relieved that the sound hadn't been the result of some catastrophic disaster that I found myself laughing along with the kids. And for a moment, I felt lucky that I was the one home with them. Miguel got to be the star, but it was my role as support staff that let me witness these special moments firsthand. This was something I could be grateful for . . . for this, and for farts, because farts are always funny.

CHAPTER TWELVE
The Acceptor

A few months after Jackson started at his new preschool, he came home with an invitation in his backpack for a mom's night out. New Jersey Kelly would have been too busy or tired to attend. But Chicago Kelly was so eager to make new friends that she accidentally showed up for the mixer a week early.

When I later showed up on the correct date, I was disappointed to realize that what I was actually desperate for was mom friends who understood the medical caregiver life. Especially as I listened to a mom complain about how her baby was getting into everything now that he could crawl. *She has no idea how lucky she is.* I wanted to be talking about doctor recommendations and medication side effects, and if one brand of orthotics was better than another, and if they did physical therapy in a clinic or at their home.

Shortly after Adelaide had been diagnosed with infantile spasms, I joined several Facebook groups for parents of children with IS. At the time I was looking for information and hope but hadn't been active in the discussions. However, after the preschool mom night, I went back to the IS group and decided to introduce myself and share our story. Comments rolled in, at first welcoming me to the group—and then one mother commented that she also lived in Chicago. Then another said she did as well.

By the following morning, both families had been invited to our home for a brunch that would take several weeks to coordinate between our children's appointments and hospitalizations. All three of our IS children were born within months of each other, none of them were walking or talking, and all were on a variety of medications. We sat around our living room with our little ones propped up on pillows or sitting in our laps.

"Who is your doctor? Do you like them?"

"What side effects did you find with that medication?"

"What do his seizures look like, and how long do they last?"

This was the conversation I'd yearned for. I was abundantly aware of how abnormal our normal had become. But with these families, our abnormal normal was shared and understood.

Becoming a part of a community was a relief. But it would take meeting Susan Axelrod to understand just how influential this community could be to my life.

Before I was even pregnant with Adelaide, I had helped coordinate a fundraising event for a nonprofit called Citizens United for Research in Epilepsy, now known as CURE Epilepsy. At the time, I'd known nothing about the organization and even less about epilepsy, but following Adelaide's diagnosis, I scoured old emails for a contact. Wouldn't you know it, they were headquartered in Chicago. What were the odds?

I'd reached out to my contact there for doctor recommendations and might have let slip why we were moving to Chicago. Specifically, the part about *Hamilton*. Their interest had certainly been piqued, as the interest of any diligent nonprofit with fundraising goals should have been. A few months after our move, CURE Epilepsy's founder

Susan Axelrod invited me to lunch. But when for one reason or another Adelaide landed herself back in the hospital, Susan offered to bring lunch to me in the hospital instead.

"Kelly? Hi, I'm Susan." She was dressed casually, with silver hair just past her shoulders, and was carrying two white bags. When she reached Adelaide lying in the hospital crib, she paused. The sides of the crib were so high that Miguel referred to it as "baby jail." Adelaide turned her head—wrapped in the signature EEG helmet of white gauze and tape—to look at the new voice. It almost looked like Susan was tearing up, but if so, she recovered before turning back to me.

"Hi Susan, it's so nice to meet you. That's Adelaide," I said, gesturing toward baby jail. "Have a seat. Sorry I don't have more comfortable chairs to offer," I joked, motioning to the commercial-grade, vinyl-upholstered hospital recliner.

"It never gets easier. Seeing the babies all hooked up." Susan's gaze had drifted back to Adelaide. "It's been over thirty years since my daughter had her first EEG, and I hate that we're still here fighting." She paused for a moment then seemed to remember the white bags she was holding. "I hope salads are okay. Figure it must be better than whatever you're getting here."

"Thank you," I said, taking the bag, "Although, the food here is significantly better than in the New Jersey hospital."

"That's right. I can't believe you are managing all this in a new city . . . and my guess is you're doing most of it on your own," she said, settling into the chair beside me.

"Yeah . . . I am. Miguel's schedule is challenging."

"I can relate. When Lauren, my daughter, was in and out of hospitals, my husband David was also consumed with work."

"Oh, what does he do?" I asked, intrigued by this commonality.

Susan didn't say anything for a moment, but her eyes crinkled at the corners. "He's a political consultant and works on presidential campaigns. He was also an advisor to President Obama." Her delivery of this world-defining information was as nonchalant as if she had said her husband was a CPA or a high school principal. Blood rushed to my cheeks. Of course I'd heard of David Axelrod, I just hadn't realized Susan was married to him.

"Oh my god. I'm so embarrassed. Of course, I didn't—I just never put that together." *She must think I'm an idiot!*

Susan laughed for the first time since entering the hospital room. "Usually, my husband is the first thing people want to talk about. This has actually been quite refreshing."

"Well, we certainly have that in common," I said, all at once relieved and in awe.

I would come to learn that it was around a kitchen table in Susan's home, alongside several other determined mothers, that CURE Epilepsy had been founded. Susan was frustrated with the conversations she was having with Lauren's doctors and several epilepsy nonprofits who were all focused on living well with epilepsy. That wasn't good enough for her: she wanted a cure. Her organization single-handedly forced epilepsy researchers and nonprofits to see curing epilepsies as a feasible goal. Having raised over $100 million in their first twenty-six years, CURE Epilepsy is the largest nongovernmental funder of epilepsy research in the world.

We visited together for an hour, talking about Adelaide and her daughter Lauren, who was my age but, due to epilepsy, was developmentally still a child. She told me about her two neurotypical sons, and I spoke about Jackson. It was wild how much we had in common, from the career she'd abandoned to care for her disabled daughter to her own loss of identity and purpose. She patiently educated me on the epilepsy landscape and her dreams of curing epilepsy so that she didn't ever have to see another child connected to an EEG again.

What would stick with me most from Susan's visit was the proof she gave of life continuing even with a devastating diagnosis. And not just for her daughter, but for Susan and her entire family. I'd dared to let myself hope. Even if Adelaide never fully recovered, even if she was never "normal," maybe we could still enjoy this life.

DURING OUR FIRST Chicago spring, which is really just more winter, Miguel and I started noticing suspicious eye flutters again and even a head drop or two. But when I called the epilepsy clinic to share my concerns, I was instructed to wait for our already scheduled EEG the following month. Even though my mommy intuition was setting off alarms, the rule follower in me was hitting the snooze button. To further complicate matters, Adelaide's doctor had informed us she would be transferring to a hospital out of state shortly after Adelaide's scheduled EEG, and we had no idea who her new doctor would be.

For a month, we watched as the eye flutters grew more pronounced and the head drops more frequent. But what was I supposed to do? If the clinic had been concerned, they would have had us come in sooner, right?

"I'm sorry, it's not good news," Adelaide's epileptologist informed us over the phone after the scheduled EEG. "It appears the infantile spasms have returned. We'll get her started on a burst of high-dose prednisone, which you can administer from home, and then you can call the epilepsy clinic to schedule a follow-up appointment."

I'd hoped we were overreacting, but I'd known better. I had a photo album on my phone full of video after video of suspicious jerks, blinks, and tremors. *Why didn't I trust myself?* There wasn't time for that kind of thinking, though. From across our dining room table, where we had taken the call on speaker phone, Miguel was rubbing his face in frustration, caught up in what appeared to be a similar internal monologue.

"What is the name of the doctor replacing you?" Miguel asked. I waited for her answer with my pen poised, ready to take down as much information as possible.

"They're still working on it. These transitions are always a challenge, but I assure you it will work out. Mr. and Mrs. Cervantes, it truly has been a pleasure treating Adelaide, and I wish your family the best."

I stared down at my notepad and the few notes I'd taken on the steroid dosing and absorbed the reality contained within my pen strokes.
If this steroid treatment was anything like the first, Adelaide would
once again become a 'roid-raging monster and likely regress even further, and as of now we didn't even have a doctor to consult regarding
side effects or effectiveness.

"Damn it!" Miguel said, shoving his chair back from the table.

Helplessness consumed me. Why was this happening? Why
couldn't we control these seizures? And why did it feel like we were
managing this on our own?

The next day, I called the hospital's scheduling line to make the
follow-up appointment.

"Okay, it looks like Adelaide's neurologist is no longer with the
hospital," the scheduler informed me.

"I know. I need to schedule an appointment with someone else. I
believe that Dr. Carwich specializes in my daughter's seizure type; I
would like to schedule an appointment with him, please."

"Dr. Carwich is booked out for several months. The first available
appointment is with Dr. Lee in June," the scheduler responded.

"That's two months away!"

"Yes, that's the first available appointment."

Deep breaths. Make her understand.

"My daughter is currently on a high-dose steroid treatment for
infantile spasms, and I need a doctor to guide me through the dosing
and tapering. We can't wait two months."

"You are welcome to call back each morning to see if there are any
cancellations," the scheduler offered.

"No. My daughter had a doctor there. She left. It is not her fault
that her doctor left. She needs to see someone next week so we can
make a plan," I insisted.

"That's just not something I can do. Would you like the appointment with Dr. Lee?"

Enraged, I hung up.

Miguel appeared beside me, a freshly dressed Adelaide held against his chest. "Did she just tell you they couldn't get Adelaide in for two months?"

"Yes." I stood up and began pacing between the kitchen and the couch. *Is this really happening? How are there no guardrails against this?* "We could try a different hospital," I suggested. Chicago was fortunate to have not one but three hospitals with highly regarded pediatric epilepsy units. However, all of Adelaide's care was currently centralized at one, and the thought of transferring it or communicating across multiple medical institutions had my head spinning.

"I think I met someone high up at the hospital when the cast sang Christmas carols there last year. Let me see if I can find the business card he gave me," Miguel said, handing me Adelaide and heading upstairs to look through the pile of papers on top of his dresser.

It was a good thought, but we had a better chance of the seizures stopping on their own than we did of my well-intentioned but easily distracted husband finding a business card he received months ago.

"We shouldn't have to ask for special treatment to get an appointment," I mumbled to myself. *We shouldn't have to fight for an appointment in the first place.*

After conceding his business card search, Miguel called the scheduling line himself, explaining who he was and who he knew. Within minutes, he was able to secure an appointment with Dr. Carwich for the following week. Meanwhile, I took advantage of new connections at CURE Epilepsy to get an appointment with a Dr. Marcuccilli at another medical system just a few days later. I was relieved we now had a plan, but while I knew no one would blame me for pulling every string available to get my daughter help, the inequity of basic access weighed heavy on my conscience.

Any relief I felt, though, would quickly wear off as the steroids transformed our sweet little girl into an irritable gremlin. I knew she needed these drugs, but I also needed her off them as soon as feasibly possible. I counted down the days to our first appointment with Dr. Marcuccilli.

When the appointment finally came, I was desperate for the man entering the clinic room with salt-and-pepper hair, bushy eyebrows, and thick glasses to just tell us what to do.

"Hi! I'm so sorry to keep you waiting," He was wearing a white doctor coat over a shirt and tie and carrying a small medical case reminiscent of what doctors once took with them on house calls. "I've been going nonstop since this morning, and my nurse just reminded me to eat lunch. I'm Dr. Marcuccilli."

"Hi, doctor. I'm Kelly, this is my husband Miguel, and this fuss-monster is Adelaide."

"Hello, Adelaide." Dr. Marcuccilli said, addressing her directly. "It is very nice to meet you." Adelaide responded to her name for a moment before returning to her wordless protests. Seemingly satisfied with the introductions, Dr. Marcuccilli turned to face the computer screen and opened Adelaide's chart. "Alright, I see she's currently being treated elsewhere. So you're looking for a second opinion?"

"Actually, we are looking for a new epileptologist." I handed him the bursting two-inch binder in which I kept all of Adelaide's test results and care summaries. Dr. Marcuccilli eagerly accepted the binder. "It's organized chronologically and separated by report type."

"This is *very* helpful, thank you." Dr. Marcuccilli said, scanning the papers within. For the first time, I felt seen and appreciated as a member of my daughter's care team. I forced down the lump forming in my throat.

Dr. Marcuccilli sat with us for a full forty-five minutes. He discussed different tests we could do, showed us what he saw in Adelaide's EEG, and briefed us on how that information could be used to treat her. He explained that whenever she had a seizure, even a small one, it was as if someone was briefly turning out the lights. Each time this happened, she had to stop and get her bearings. She had to reprocess whatever she had been focusing on, if she remembered at all. To a developing brain, this stopping and starting was devastating.

No one had ever taken the time to explain Adelaide's seizures to us and certainly not in a way that we could understand. Miguel and I looked at each other, desperate but hopeful, the way only two parents who have sat in innumerable plastic clinic room chairs could. This doctor was different.

"Should you decide to have Adelaide treated by me, I would want to get her in for a follow-up EEG in a couple of weeks to see where the seizures are at and to decide the best course of future treatment."

"Thank you so much. We're seeing another doctor in a few days, but I feel fairly confident that we will be back to see you," I said, squeezing Miguel's hand.

"That's great, well, just call my office and let me know." Then he turned to Adelaide. "We have a lot of work to do, little girl."

His parting words stuck with me. "Did you hear what Dr. Marcuccilli said when we were leaving?" I asked Miguel on the drive home.

"About the tests he wants to order?" Miguel asked, distracted by a city bus pulling out in front of him.

"That and how we have a lot of work to do. He actually wants to try and figure her out."

"Right, not just throw darts at a medication list and hope one works."

"Exactly!"

I turned around in my seat to look at Adelaide, who was much calmer now that we were in a moving car. I squeezed her tiny, socked foot. The connection I felt to the miniature human before me was so strong I might have thought we were still biologically attached. Lesson learned. I would not be settling for her medical care ever again.

DURING THIS SECOND round of steroids, if Adelaide wasn't in motion, she was screaming. It's amazing I didn't wear tread marks into the floor from wheeling her stroller around our home. When she woke at four in the morning inconsolable, I would strap her into her car seat and drive around the neighborhood so that Miguel could still get some sleep.

"Please don't leave. I can't do this anymore," I begged Mom through tears as she and Dad were getting ready to go back home after a long-weekend visit.

"She won't be on the steroids forever. You can do this, I know you can." She enveloped me in a hug that I never wanted to end. "I love you, and I am so proud of you."

I knew she was right: this phase wouldn't last forever. But I no longer trusted that whatever was coming next would be any better. Thankfully, after several weeks, Adelaide's tests showed the steroids had stopped the spasms along with the damaging hypsarrhythmia (for now, anyway). And after several more weeks, her irritability finally waned as well—just in time to enjoy a beautiful Chicago summer and what would become a glorious stretch of three seizure-free months.

After a family dinner at a casual outdoor restaurant overlooking Lake Michigan, we walked along the beach and watched the sun set over the city. Jackson and Miguel found a forgotten football and were running routes, faking touchdown celebrations and tackling each other in the sand. Adelaide and I watched the boys play from a grassy hill above the beach.

The sunlight filtering through the trees created a spotlight effect, highlighting the blonde sprout of a ponytail on top of Adelaide's head as she sat in her stroller. Her face was still full from the steroids, and everywhere else, her rolls had rolls. She was just perfectly squishable in her red, white, and blue–striped cotton summer dress. So I squished her . . . and then she smiled at me, her dark hazel eyes crinkling at the corners.

It had been months since she had smiled. The infantile spasms and steroids had once again hidden her personality in the recesses of her mind. But there she was, bathed in the golden summer light and smiling. Not just smiling, but smiling *at me*. Having a nonverbal, nonmobile child requires everything of you. When they can't say "mama," let alone "I love you," well, one smile—one perfect, open-mouthed, toothy grin—is all of those words and more.

NOT EVERY LIFE change arrives with the immediacy of a phone call or fateful appointment. Some take time and are only noticed in hindsight. For example, I never woke up one morning and thought to myself, *This is our life now, and that's okay*. But at some point, *I* was okay.

Similarly, I'm not sure when we went from thinking we were only going to be in Chicago for one year to buying a condo down the street from the house we were renting. But that happened too. Our new home was a modern Chicago duplex with two long and narrow floors. On the main floor was an open living room and kitchen with floor-to-ceiling windows looking onto Armitage Avenue, a busy street in the Bucktown neighborhood. Just past the kitchen was Adelaide's room, a bathroom, and Miguel's and my bedroom. Downstairs was a second living space, along with Jackson's bedroom and bathroom.

The most important criteria we had looked for was that Adelaide's and our bedrooms were on the same level as the kitchen and living room. Adelaide was physically and cognitively delayed, but her growth had not been impeded. She was the same size as an average two-year old, but incapable of supporting herself. Carrying her up and down stairs was only going to get more difficult. Fortunately, this condo checked every imaginable box. It was perfect for our family, and I had mentally decorated every room before we even signed the mortgage.

Adelaide's second birthday doubled as our housewarming party. I knew we had to celebrate her for the fighter she was, so I traded out the previous year's cutesy pink and gold décor for a powerful red, blue, and gold Wonder Woman theme. Alongside our new epilepsy friends, we celebrated Adelaide's strength and spunk.

The day stood in stark contrast to the prior year's festivities when I had fought against Adelaide's disabled reality, clinging to what was still possible even if not probable. I looked across the party to where Susan and David Axelrod stood smiling, awash in sunlight, and eating birthday cake. Again I wondered if we could be happy with this life. What would a happy life *with* seizures, *with* regular hospitalizations, *with* therapy equipment look like? I thought of the way Jackson saw and interacted with his sister, whether he was cuddling on the couch or playing with a whoopee cushion. He was content to be with Adelaide as she was.

I wanted to be able to do that too. But it meant accepting Adelaide's disabilities were a part of her, and that was proving more challenging than I cared to admit. Up until Adelaide, I had viewed life as a series of milestones on a checklist:

- Go to college
- Build a career
- Get married
- Start a family

How would Adelaide ever complete her own list if she was still struggling to achieve the milestones on that two-month checklist we'd received at the pediatrician's office two years ago? Accepting Adelaide's reality was going to require that I completely upend the value system I'd based my life upon. For as long as I could remember, I assessed my worth based on what I accomplished. On whether I earned the free pizza from the summer reading program or made the dean's list. If Adelaide never walked or talked, if she was dependent on others for the entirety of her life, did that life still have value?

The answer was obvious.

For one thing, I could feel the value that she brought to my life every day. Being Adelaide's mother had enlarged my heart to epic proportions. I felt more deeply, loved more passionately, lived more fully, *because* she was my daughter. I saw the effect she had on her brother as he empathetically interacted with other children with disabilities at her birthday party or on playdates. And on Miguel as he used his *Hamilton* platform to raise awareness and money for epilepsy research. Adelaide made all of us better people.

Initially, I had viewed accepting her disabilities as akin to giving up. The goal was to live typically, right? Awash in déjà vu, I remembered how growing up I'd felt that sameness was valued, but it had actually been difference that was feared. The parallels were difficult to ignore. Except now, instead of coloring inside the lines of culture and religion, I was perpetuating ideals of physical and intellectual ability. Author and teacher Heather Lanier wrote about this beautifully in her book *Raising a Rare Girl*. "Bodily difference is charming so long as it doesn't interfere with Normal. Or if it does interfere with Normal—if it is a Disability—it's charming so long as it becomes history, a tale to offer as inspiration rather than a real life to live. Disability is okay if it's overcome."

It was becoming clear that Adelaide wasn't going to outgrow or overcome her disabilities. Instead, I was the one who needed to grow and accept Adelaide as she was. I turned to the disability and epilepsy communities to see how I could embrace Adelaide's differences while still helping her to grow stronger and healthier. No concept helped guide me more than inchstones. It's a basic notion, really: instead of focusing on major milestones like walking and talking, you acknowledge all the seemingly smaller achievements along the way. The ones that are often taken for granted when parenting a neurotypical child. I wasn't giving up on Adelaide ever reaching certain milestones; instead, I was choosing to celebrate all that Adelaide *could* do, noting the progress she *was* making. My daily life would be forever changed by focusing on her quality of life over the quantity of boxes checked.

Adelaide's physical therapist, Lisa, was at our house for their regular Thursday session. They stretched and worked on core strength and head control, and then toward the end of the hour Lisa decided to try putting Adelaide in her therapy walker. Adelaide had been fitted for the equipment just before her infantile spasms had returned, and it had sat collecting dust in the corner of our living room ever since. I retrieved the walker while Lisa secured Adelaide's leg braces and tied on her adorable navy and pink New Balance sneakers. Then we strapped Adelaide into the walker, which resembled a wheelchair but instead of a seat had supports at her chest, under her arms, and between her legs to keep her upright.

"Are you ready to walk, Adelaide?"

Adelaide stood in the contraption, trying to figure out if it was less effort to lift her thumb all the way to her mouth or to bring her mouth down to her raised thumb. The collar around her neck, which helped with head support, was further restricting her efforts. Lisa pushed the walker slowly, and Adelaide let her feet drag below her.

"This is your leg," Lisa said, touching Adelaide's calf, "and this is your foot." Lisa gently stomped Adelaide's foot on our wood floors. "Now you're going to take a step." As Lisa moved the walker forward, she helped Adelaide move her foot forward. "Now, where's your other foot?" she asked, rocking the walker back and forth to help Adelaide feel the pressure on her feet. With Lisa's next small push of the walker, Adelaide brought her left foot up to meet her right—on her own.

"That's it!" squealed Lisa.

"Adelaide, you did it!" I ran to her and kissed her head.

Adelaide was more relieved that she had stopped moving so she could once again attempt to connect her thumb with her mouth. She wasn't walking—she hadn't even taken an independent step—but from my reaction you might have thought that she had performed a tap dance. Adelaide had brought one foot to meet the other, something she had never done before. It was an inchstone that I would capture on video when she did it again moments later and proceed to share with everyone the way I had the video of Jackson's first steps.

That day, Adelaide showed me that accepting where she was developmentally and focusing on her progress, regardless of its perceived pace, was the antithesis of giving up. We were still working and fighting for each inchstone, and by releasing my preconceived expectations of milestone checklists, I could remain optimistic and encouraged. She would make progress an inchstone at a time to the extent her body was able.

Dr. Marcuccilli's voice echoed in my mind. *We have a lot of work to do, little girl.*

CHAPTER THIRTEEN
The Survivalist

It had been a week since Adelaide's second birthday party, and I had yet to take down the Wonder Woman decorations. At some point, I hoped they would just start to blend into our regular décor, negating the need to remove them. Miguel had returned from taking Jackson to school and was sitting in the kitchen while I wheeled a fussy Adelaide around the apartment in her stroller.

Should I cancel her occupational therapy appointment? When was her last poop? Could she be constipated? What should she wear today? I thought, turning the corner with her stroller.

"Kelly, stop. Does she look pale to you?" Miguel asked.

I walked around the stroller to get a better look at Adelaide's face. At first glance, she appeared to finally be asleep—except that her usually flushed cheeks and lips were chalk white.

"Adelaide," I said, trying to rouse her.

No response.

I quickly unfastened the straps on the stroller and picked her up. She was a rag doll, her head flopping onto my shoulder. "Oh my god."

Miguel took control. "We need to get her to the hospital now."

I don't know why we didn't call 911, but in our panic, we decided to drive her to the hospital ourselves. After clicking Adelaide into her car seat, I crouched beside her in between our minivan's captain seats.

"Hey, my love, stay with me, okay? Mommy is right here." I spoke to Adelaide in the hope that her subconscious could still hear me.

"Is she breathing?" Miguel asked, pulling out of our garage into the alley.

I placed a finger under Adelaide's nose and felt the faint brush of warm air coordinating with a slight visible rise of her chest.

"Yes, but barely."

"Find a closer hospital." Miguel instructed.

I pulled out my phone. "There's one by the high school near Western Ave."

Without a seatbelt, or even a real seat, I tried to maintain my balance while keeping watch on the rise and fall of Adelaide's chest. Until I didn't see it rise.

"Adelaide? *Adelaide*! She's not breathing!" I screamed.

"We're almost there!" Miguel pulled into a cul-de-sac entrance marked "EMERGENCY." With Adelaide in my arms, I ran through the sliding glass doors and into a small waiting room.

"My baby isn't breathing! Please, someone help! She's not breathing!" A nurse came around the corner, took one look at Adelaide in my arms and rushed us back to a large triage room with individual hospital beds separated by curtains. She directed me to one of the stalls, and I placed Adelaide on the bed.

A doctor and two nurses pushed into the curtained space, and I stepped back, not knowing what to do or where to go.

"What happened? Did she choke? Is she allergic to anything? What is her name?" A voice yelled out toward me.

"Her name is Adelaide. I don't know what happened. She was fussy and then she wasn't, and we brought her here. She has epilepsy and is hypotonic." I answered in the direction of the faceless voice. There were so many people surrounding her bed I couldn't make out what was going on. All I could see of my daughter was one tiny, pink-socked foot in a very large bed.

"Hi, I just need to ask you a few questions." A nurse appeared next to me with a clipboard offering me a tissue. I took the tissue as Miguel ran in from the parking lot.

"What's going on? Is she okay?" Miguel stood on his tiptoes trying to get a better look inside the curtained stall.

"I don't know" was all I could choke out.

"I'll come back," the nurse said. "I think your wife needs you," she softly suggested to Miguel, who stood frozen, staring into the room that held our daughter and the bustling medical professionals.

Miguel turned to me, and we clung to each other. Time ceased to exist. At some point, a man, who I assumed was a doctor by his white coat, approached us.

"Are you Mom and Dad?" he asked.

"Yes," Miguel answered.

"We were able to stabilize your daughter."

"She's okay? Can we see her?" I asked.

"You can. She's currently receiving additional oxygen support, which seems to be helping . . ."

I ran toward the pink-socked foot. Adelaide was awake and sucking her thumb with an oxygen cannula in her nose. The color was back in her cheeks and her lips. She looked like my baby girl, my Adelaideybug. Miguel rubbed her hand and lightly squeezed each part of her body, as if to make sure they were all still there. From the other side of the bed, I ran my fingers through her hair and started singing a song I had made up for her when she was a newborn.

"Adelaidey aidey baby, Adelaidey aidey baby, Adelaide, Adelaide, Adelaidey Grace."

Whether or not the song calmed her, it certainly helped me. For the first time, in all her many health scares and hospital visits, I hadn't been sure she would survive. I don't know that words exist to clearly describe that level of fear, the utter intractability of the situation. With each repetition of the song though, I felt stronger, more stable, and more in control.

"Excuse me, I'm sorry." The nurse with the clipboard was back. "I just need to get that information from you. Also, the doctor doesn't feel we can properly care for her here and wants to know where you would like her transferred.

Miguel kissed Adelaide's forehead and went into the hall to speak with the nurse.

"Mommy's here, Adelaidey. I'm not going anywhere, okay?"

Adelaide turned her head to look at me for a moment before returning to her thumb. That was good enough for me. I just kept running my fingers through her hair and singing.

Over the next five days, Dr. Marcuccilli's team tested her brain, heart, lungs, blood, and urine. But no one could determine a cause for what they were calling an ALTE, or an apparent life-threatening event. What was as shocking as it was terrifying was that they didn't think it had been related to a seizure. Seizures I at least sort of understood, but something *new*? How could we prevent it from happening again? What were the signs to watch out for? How was I supposed to wrest control back from luck if I didn't know what I was defending against?

Before Adelaide was born, I thought that medical mysteries were rare, that the answers were out there, and you just had to find a Dr. House or Watson to diagnose you. Not so. Without a known underlying cause, we were left treating Adelaide's growing list of symptoms, and that was not proving effective. It meant we had no idea what to expect for Adelaide's future; there was no prognosis, no road map. I might as well have been driving a race car blindfolded. It wasn't a question of if we would crash again, but when. I just had to hope that we had enough safety measures in place to survive.

With Adelaide off the additional oxygen and with no other tests to conduct, we were sent home with instructions to keep a close eye on our very adorable but very unstable time bomb of a daughter. If not for Dr. Marcuccilli ordering us a pulse oximeter, a device that measures blood oxygen levels and heart rate through a monitor taped to a finger or toe, I'm not sure I would have ever slept again.

"MOMMY, CAN I have a brother?" Jackson asked, his chin covered in spaghetti sauce.

Someone might as well have reached inside my chest and squeezed my heart, à la *Temple of Doom*. Had I made it through a near-death experience with one child only to be taken out at a family dinner by the other? I took a bite of pasta to buy myself time.

"It doesn't really work that way. You don't get to choose if you get a brother or a sister." I was avoiding his question, and he knew it.

"Okay, can I have a brother *or* another sister then? But one that doesn't have epilepsy and can play with me?"

The vise around my heart tightened.

"I wish we could say yes, but we don't know why Adelaide is sick, and there is a chance that if we had another baby, they would be sick like Adelaide. I promise that I'm trying to figure it out though." Jackson seemed satisfied with my answer for now.

"I'm full, can I have my treat?"

"You're full for dinner but not your treat?"

"Uh-huh."

"Three more bites, please." Dinner was a constant negotiation with Jackson. For a moment, I was grateful for Adelaide's G-tube. There was no complaining, fighting, or bartering when food was pumped directly into her stomach. .

Jackson's question about a sibling had caught me off guard, but it wasn't as if Miguel and I hadn't been thinking about this as well. We had always planned on having two children. Correction: we had always thought we would have two *healthy* children and that they would have each other after we died. But what if Adelaide died, leaving Jackson alone? Or what if she outlived us, and Jackson was tasked with her care?

Not having an overarching diagnosis left us questioning whether our genes could even produce another healthy baby. Our current track record of one healthy child for every three pregnancies was not encouraging. Had Jackson been a miracle?

In my quest for answers, I enrolled Adelaide in the Undiagnosed Diseases Network, a research program funded by the National Institutes of Health whose mission is to help patients on their diagnostic journey. Mom met me at the UDN site at Duke University in North Carolina where we spent a week meeting with doctors, holding Adelaide as she went through test after test and exam after exam. The scientists in the program agreed that whatever was causing Adelaide's issues was genetic, but didn't know if it had been inherited or was another unlucky lightning strike like Elvis's condition had been. Regardless, they promised to continue following up on the few leads they had found.

Since we had exhausted our diagnostic options, all we could do now was wait, either for a scientific breakthrough or for Adelaide to develop a new symptom that gave us another clue. Now my focus had to be keeping Adelaide stable. Perhaps if there wasn't another medical catastrophe negating her progress, she might even be able to develop new skills. Being stable was also imperative if we had any hope of sending her to school someday. I knew the school would look different from anything I had initially envisioned, but I wanted her to have that experience, to learn, play, and make friends.

Good lord, did we all need some good friends right about now.

CHAPTER FOURTEEN
The Friend

I watched so many of my high school classmates go away to college with a plan to return to Omaha afterward and raise children among their extended family. I swore I wouldn't do that. After all, my parents hadn't raised my brother and I near their parents, and it had been fine. Admittedly, I had been a little jealous of the relationships some of my friends had with their cousins, but I got to travel all over the country to visit my family. My parents hadn't been able to rely on their parents for babysitting, but I had loved the babysitters they hired and even invited them to my birthday parties.

"Just because it was fine doesn't mean it was easy," my mother would later admit to me. And that was with two healthy, neurotypical children. Parenting under any circumstances is a marathon: you start out full of hope and energy and by the time your kids (hopefully) leave the house, you are exhausted, drained, and your body doesn't work as well as it did at the start. But the race I had embarked on wasn't a typical parenting marathon. This felt more like being thrown into an Ironman Triathlon without any training.

While my epilepsy mom friends were amazing, they were navigating their own chaos, and for all the reasons I was unreliable, so were they. Just preparing to leave the house with Adelaide was its own gauntlet. How long would we be gone? What did I need to bring? What could go wrong? What did I need to bring in case something did go wrong? Staying home was safer and easier. And by easier, I mean I experienced less anxiety.

What I wanted was a village. I wanted more people I could lean on for help. But where to start? And who would want to be friends with someone as needy as me? Access to *Hamilton* tickets and backstage tours only went so far.

Instead of branching out, I turned to a consistent friend who, at the moment, needed me almost as much as I needed her. Regardless of how often we saw each other, Courtney and I had the kind of friendship where if the other person was struggling, we showed up. And right then we were both struggle bus ticket holders.

Six days after Adelaide's initial epilepsy diagnosis and two days after Miguel landed *Hamilton*, Courtney had experienced a world-altering event of her own. Her mom, Lori, had passed away due to complications from mast cell activation syndrome, a rare and chronic illness where the mast cells in a person's immune system inappropriately activate, leading to a range of allergy-like symptoms caused by an overactivation of histamines.

Courtney was understandably devastated by the loss of her mother, but the loss cut even deeper; they also shared the same rare disease. So when Lori died, Courtney didn't just lose her mother: she lost her best friend, her advocate, and the only other person she knew who could relate to and understand her complicated health. Courtney and Lori had been undiagnosed until Courtney finally found answers in an online community during her challenging pregnancy. When the rest of Courtney's friends struggled to understand why she couldn't be around this smell, or eat that food, or had to cancel at the last minute due to a bad reaction, Lori always got it. Now Courtney didn't have anyone who understood her health either.

I'm sure I didn't always say the right thing to Courtney, but what mattered was that I was there. From my living room in Chicago to hers in Westchester, we checked in with each other every night after our kids had been put to bed. I listened as she told me things she wished she could share with her mom, from a worsening symptom to how her son was growing.

Meanwhile, Courtney became my medical chaperone, encouraging me to find the best medical team for Adelaide, giving me advice on how to get what I needed from insurance, and reminding me that a parent's intuition is not to be trifled with. We also shared our more light-hearted moments and joked about our husbands, as friends do. But perhaps what I valued most was that no topic was off-limits, no feeling or action was judged.

I need something else to do besides counting Adelaide's seizures and fighting with our insurance. But I am the least dependable person that exists. I can't even volunteer at Jackson's school for fear of Adelaide landing back in the hospital, I texted Courtney one night.

Why don't you reach out to CURE Epilepsy and see what you can do for them? If anyone is going to understand your time constraints, they will, Courtney typed back. *And if they don't, you don't want to be working with them anyway.*

Courtney was nothing if not straightforward. Her advice led me to connect with CURE Epilepsy and Susan Axelrod in a more direct and meaningful way. I spoke at fundraising events, joined the board of directors, and would eventually host their podcast, *Seizing Life*. Finally, I had found an additional purpose outside our home—one that allowed me to feel useful and add value to the world as Kelly, in addition to as a mom and a wife. Best yet, Adelaide was always welcome at meetings and events.

OUR SECOND YEAR in Chicago was now underway, and Jackson had started kindergarten at a large public school. He was outgoing and friendly and excited to make new friends. But I also knew it was only a matter of time before he understood that most children didn't have to wait for their sister to be done having a seizure before their mommy could get them a snack. To help normalize our family life, we asked Jackson's teacher if we could bring Adelaide into Jackson's class. Maybe we could prevent Jackson's future discomfort by educating his class-mates upfront.

"Hi, this is my sister Adelaide, and she has epilepsy. Sometimes she has seizures, and her eyes get really big, and her arm will shoot out straight, and sometimes she cries. She can't walk or talk, but she eats her food through this tube in her tummy, and she's really cute, and I love her a lot," Jackson proudly told his class. "Any questions?"

Over a dozen small hands shot up in the air, and Jackson puffed up with the responsibility of being able to choose whose question he answered first. He pointed to a girl sitting right in front of him.

"Why does she have epilepsy?"

"Well, we're not really sure," I said. "Something doesn't work quite right in her brain, but you don't have to worry; it's not contagious."

"Will she ever get better?"

"We're trying everything we can, but right now, there is no cure for epilepsy, so we really don't know," Miguel answered.

"What's important to remember is that Adelaide is just like you and me, and she still wants friends and for people to be nice to her," I added. "Whether someone wears glasses, or needs a wheelchair to get around, has difficulty speaking, or has epilepsy, they are still people with feelings. We are all different and unique in our own ways, and that is pretty great because the world would be super boring if we were all the same."

"I have glasses!"

"I saw someone in a wheelchair yesterday!"

"Has Adelaide seen *Hamilton*?"

It was hard to tell how much Jackson's classmates absorbed in the moment. However, they never ceased to impress me. Whenever I brought Adelaide to pick up Jackson after school, a semicircle would form around her.

"Hi, Adelaide!"

"I know you can't say anything back, but I just wanted to say hi."

"Jackson's right, she is really cute."

Jackson beamed with pride as he stood next to Adelaide's stroller during these post-school meet and greets. For me, they brought an unexpected peace as I realized how much I had yearned for Adelaide to experience kindness over pity. It's incredible how a little knowledge can foster a wealth of empathy.

Unfortunately, things weren't as simple as making sure Jackson had friends who understood his family. Adelaide was continuing to rack up frequent-flier points at the hospital, and when I was with her, and Miguel was at the theater, Jackson was left with a rotation of babysitters and family friends. One afternoon I surprised him at school pickup, leaving Miguel in the hospital with Adelaide.

"Are you back for good? Is Adelaide home?!" Jackson asked, leaping into my arms when he saw me.

"No, I have to head back to the hospital after I put you to bed. Ms. Susan will be here if you need anything after that." Jackson's face fell. He didn't say another word until we were nearly home.

"How come I always have to have the babysitter? Why can't you stay here and Adelaide gets the babysitter?" In the rearview mirror, I saw his eyes well with tears.

Hold it together, Kelly.

"It doesn't work that way, monkey, I'm so sorry," I responded, clinging to the steering wheel for support. There was no way he could understand, and he shouldn't freaking have to!

When we were home, I knelt down to help Jackson untie his shoes.

"We have the worst family," Jackson mumbled just loud enough for me to hear.

I looked into his eyes. "Listen, you have *every right* to be sad and angry. But try not to be angry at Mommy or Daddy or Adelaide, okay? We are all just trying our best." I wanted to sweep him up in my arms and hold him in a rocking chair, kiss his boo-boos, and make everything okay. Tell him it would all work out, that this was just for now. But I couldn't.

He nodded his head in agreement but refused to look at me.

"You can be angry at epilepsy, though," I offered. "In fact, you know how I don't like it when you say you 'hate' something? Well, you can hate epilepsy. I do. You can even *say* you hate epilepsy." At this he finally looked up at me.

"Yeah, our family *hates* epilepsy, right, Mommy?" A rebellious glint sparkled in his eye.

"You got that right, monkey." I swallowed him in a massive hug before leading him to the other room to pick out a board game and get in some snuggles before I would have to leave him again.

I felt trapped in a twisted reenactment of *Sophie's Choice* where I was repeatedly forced to sacrifice Jackson's emotional well-being for Adelaide's physical health. Unsure of how to break the cycle, I started focusing on getting Jackson better support. I found him a therapist who he called his feelings doctor. He liked having a doctor that was just his, similar to how Adelaide had hers. We also started planning special dates where Miguel and I would take Jackson somewhere without Adelaide—though we kept the plans a surprise to prevent additional heartache in case Adelaide's health sabotaged them. If there were awards for the verbal gymnastic routines we pulled off so that Jackson didn't blame his sister for his disappointments, our medal count would rival Simone Biles's.

However, even with these additional efforts. Jackson still struggled when Adelaide went into the hospital.

I wish we lived near family so Jackson could stay with Grandma or Nana instead of feeling like we are always leaving him, I texted Courtney. *All of this sucks, but it sucks extra hard that we have to do it alone.*

I wish we lived closer and could help, Courtney responded.

Me too. What was left unsaid was how Courtney's health had been slipping under the stress of losing her mother. It was no longer safe for her to travel.

What if you made it fun? Could he have a sleepover at a friend's house instead of having a babysitter at your house?

Jackson may have only been in kindergarten, but he'd had his first sleepovers at the age of three when we were scrambling for help during Adelaide's month-long infantile spasms admission.

In theory, but I haven't had time to set up playdates or get to know the families in his class. Also it feels weird to be like—hey that playdate was awesome, can my kid live with you for a couple days?

Are there any kids he talks about more than others?

Yeah, Henry. He's been begging for a playdate with him for weeks.

So call Henry's mom tomorrow, Courtney directed.

Okay, I typed back, knowing full well I wouldn't do it.

I wanted to call her, for Jackson. But social anxiety had rendered me awkward and incapable. I was learning to accept Adelaide as she was, I was finding moments of joy amidst the stress, but how could I expect a medical normie to do the same? Our life was a lot, and I felt guilty bringing anyone else into our chaos.

Henry's mom, however, had other plans.

It was an unseasonably warm afternoon in April when Henry's mother Jenny finally got my attention at afternoon pickup.

"Henry won't stop talking about Jackson." She looked at Jackson and ruffled the hair on his head. "Since it's so nice out, I'm having some moms over this afternoon for drinks on our deck. The kids will probably just run around and terrorize my house. You should come."

My heart raced. I wouldn't know any of these women, and Miguel had to go to work which meant I would have to bring Adelaide. Nope, couldn't do it.

"Thank you, but if it's okay can I just drop Jackson off?" Jackson's eyes widened. He began jumping next to me in excitement. "Clearly, Jackson approves," I said, laughing. Win-win!

"No. You're coming too." Jenny was smiling, but her tone made it clear she had made up her mind . . . for both of us. She was also standing in the middle of the sidewalk we needed to take home, not letting me pass.

"I'd have to bring my daughter with me. She has epilepsy, and if we're outside she can overheat . . ." I explained.

"I'll take care of it," Jenny said confidently.

"She can get fussy. Really, I don't want her to ruin the afternoon." *Is she being obtuse on purpose?*

"We'll figure it out. I'll see you in an hour!" Jenny yelled the last part over her shoulder as she walked toward her car where Henry and her nine-year-old daughter Nadia were waiting.

"What just happened?" I asked, more to myself than Jackson, as we walked away from the school.

"We're going to Henry's!" Jackson squealed.

We arrived a little early, in part because I couldn't take Jackson asking me how many more minutes until we were going to Henry's, but also because I figured if we got there early, we could leave early.

While the kids wreaked havoc in Jenny's basement, the moms sat on the deck enjoying cocktails. I introduced myself and made small talk, using Adelaide as an adorable distraction if I didn't know what to say. I just needed to last a little bit longer, and then it would be acceptable to leave. Once Jenny was sure that everyone had a seat and a drink, she finally sat down herself.

"Can I hold Adelaide?" she asked.

Had I heard her right? New people never asked to hold Adelaide. I imagined they were afraid they would hurt her or induce a seizure. Her hypotonia also made her seem much more fragile than she was.

"Sure . . ." I responded, wiping a little drool from Adelaide's mouth before unclipping the stroller straps and handing her to Jenny.

If few people asked to hold Adelaide, then even fewer looked comfortable with her in their arms. But Jenny managed her with ease, and when Adelaide expressed that she'd had enough, Jenny understood and placed her back in her stroller. When it looked like Adelaide was getting flushed from being outside, Jenny brought out a fan and made a few ladies move to be sure Adelaide was sitting squarely in the shade. *Who is this woman?* Outside of our home, I had grown used to apologizing for all our additional needs, for all the additional space we took up.

"Do you mind if I take off her socks? I think it will help cool her down," Jenny asked.

"Uh, okay." Had it been anyone else, I probably would have taken offense that a stranger thought they knew my daughter's needs better than me, but Jenny was bending over backward to accommodate us.

"There, that's better," she said to Adelaide before taking a closer look at her tiny feet. "Your feet are so puffy; god, they must hurt!"

"They're always like that," I said, answering on Adelaide's behalf. "Some days are worse than others. Not sure why, maybe her dysautonomia?"

"My feet get like this too; I have lupus. It feels better when I rub them a bit." And so, right there in front of her friends, she began giving my two-year-old daughter a foot massage.

"Remind me what lupus is?" I asked.

"Oh, just one of the shitty autoimmune diseases I have. When my flare-ups are bad, they can land me in the hospital. My doctor told me I had to stop working a couple years ago, so I went on disability." She was rolling her eyes about it all as if it wasn't devastating, but I recognized this technique as if we'd pulled it from the same book. She was down-playing her experiences because she didn't want anyone feeling sorry for her.

"I miss making more money than my husband and telling him to piss off whenever I buy something he says we don't need," Jenny laughed. Actually, it was more of a cackle—but contagious all the same.

The pieces fell into place from there. She understood disability and illness. She understood what it felt like to have your ability to work taken away from you. She also knew how to have a really good time within life's limitations. I thanked my lucky Chicago Public School stars that Henry and Jackson had been placed in the same kindergarten class.

Except when she was slinging exaggerated scowls of disgust at friends for taking themselves too seriously, Jenny was usually smiling. *This* was the kind of energy I needed in my life: understanding and honest with a whip-smart sense of humor. She also wasn't fazed by Miguel being Hamilton, although she wouldn't give up an opportunity to tease me about it either.

"Julie was totally masturbating over Miguel this morning at drop-off," Jenny told me while we waited to pick up our kids one afternoon.

"Excuse me?" I had heard her, I just couldn't believe she'd said it.

"Oh, please, you know all these moms are checking out Daddy Hamilton."

Proper and appropriate she was not, but I didn't want someone to coddle me. I needed somebody real—and maybe a little crass—to pick my ass up when I stumbled. Before the end of the school year, Adelaide was back in the hospital for a few days, and this time I asked Jenny to pick Jackson up after school.

"I'll ask a babysitter or friends to bring him home after dinner," I told her.

"Uh, no you won't. You're going to leave him here. He can stay the night in our guest room. Just have Miguel drop off an overnight bag," she directed.

"Okay, thank you." I smiled, imagining the face Jenny was giving me through the phone. "Jackson will be so excited. Miguel can pick him up in the morning before school."

"Why? I can just take him to school."

"Well, I imagine his father would like to see him even if I can't," I reminded her.

"Fine. Give our girl shuggies from me."

"Shuggies?"

"Yeah, sugar, shuggies, c'mon Cervantes!" Even while I was sitting in a hospital room, she wasn't going to let me feel sorry for myself.

After that, Jackson rarely had a babysitter when Adelaide was in the hospital. Jenny's house became his second home, and Jenny like a second mom. Okay, so I hadn't made the first move like I had told Courtney I would, but I did find my village—a highly unconventional, no-bullshit, medically empathetic, and always supportive village.

CHAPTER FIFTEEN
The Advocate

After a second life-threatening episode, this time featuring an ambulance ride to a hospital trauma room where an epinephrine shot had been required to restart her heart, we added another symptom to Adelaide's medical mystery list: mast cell activation syndrome. The same rare disease that Courtney had, the same disease that had taken her mom Lori's life. It had been Courtney, of course, that pointed me in this direction and helped me connect with the only MCAS specialist in Chicago. I didn't have the time or mental bandwidth to even consider the odds of this latest coincidence.

Dr. Talbot happened to work at the same hospital as Dr. Marcuccilli, and they were willing to work together, without me acting as a middleman, to try and find a treatment that could prevent future life-threatening incidents. I can't emphasize how rare this is. Typically, doctors operate in silos, only concerned with the system they specialize in. But not only were these doctors at the same hospital, they were willing to collaborate on Adelaide's care. If it weren't for the circumstances, I might have even felt lucky.

In order to treat Adelaide's newly diagnosed MCAS, we agreed to try IV infusions that required her to spend the majority of two days in the hospital's infusion clinic every three weeks. This eventually led to having an IV port surgically implanted in her chest like a patient who is undergoing chemotherapy. This way, we didn't have to keep torturing her with IV placements in her hands, arms, or feet. The treatments didn't do much for her seizures, but we immediately saw a decrease in her fussiness, the redness in her face, and rashes that appeared around her mouth. With many of her mast cell symptoms under control, we saw a major improvement in Adelaide's quality of life.

In the last year and a half, I had come such a long way as Adelaide's advocate. I thought about how proud Lori would be of me, remembering an email she sent me just before she died: *Do not assume that someone else knows more than you, just because it is a doctor or a nurse who says they need to do something—or need to do something in a certain way. If you know it isn't right for Addie, you need to have the fight. She will need you to represent her best interests now, as there is no one else to do so. Remember, you know her better than anyone.*

At the time, I couldn't imagine going toe-to-toe with a doctor. I didn't have a medical degree and understood very little about Adelaide's conditions. The doctors were the experts, and I would do what they said, but it was sweet of her to think that I was smart enough to question them. Still, her words had stayed with me.

Have the fight.

In those early days, I was constantly questioning myself, not the doctors. I had stumbled along, blindly following their recommendations, until it became clear that Adelaide would not be one of the lucky children who responded to the frontline treatments. Only then, as Miguel and I watched the doctors become less confident, and as we realized there was no specific medical protocol for drug-resistant epilepsy, did Lori's words take on new meaning.

It started small: I had insisted that my immobile and lethargic daughter could undergo an MRI without sedation. "Schedule an appointment without sedation and one with, and if we don't need the second one you can cancel it," I'd insisted. We didn't need the second appointment.

Ha ha, losers! I know it wasn't a contest, but still, being right felt so good.

I studied Adelaide's test results, compared them with the prior ones, and then asked questions. I allowed myself to find comfort in hospital life. Like Alice stepping through a looking glass, what was once foreign was now commonplace. I became conversational, if not fluent, in the medical vernacular. I learned what accommodations we could request, where to get the best cup of coffee, and which bathroom offered the most privacy. I knew what time to expect the residents, when rounds would be for each doctor on service, and which nurses would send me home with the best syringes.

I couldn't have labeled the different lobes of the brain, and there weren't any fancy letters after my name, but my knowledge increased, and so did my confidence. I began to joke that I had a PhD in Adelaide. Being Adelaide's advocate ignited something within me.

Omaha Kelly had moved 1,500 miles away instead of confronting friends' beliefs she'd disagreed with. Boston Kelly had been willing to sacrifice her dreams for the illusion of security. New York Kelly had blamed herself for abuse that had been skillfully disguised as opportunity. But Chicago Kelly was stronger. Or maybe it was easier to advocate on someone else's behalf, or I was tired of watching my daughter seize, or I finally realized that they call it "practicing" medicine for a reason. I had learned that medicine is not one-size-fits-all, that doctors are taught that if they hear hooves to look for a horse, not a zebra. Meaning, the answer is probably common and not rare. But Adelaide *was* a zebra, and someone needed to remind the doctors that a horse's saddle, bridle, and shoes were not going to fit her.

This job as Adelaide's advocate, that I had so thoroughly resented two years prior, had become more fulfilling than any of my previous careers. Of course, I wished Adelaide was healthy, but I couldn't imagine another life's purpose ever rivaling this one. That's not to say I didn't feel daunted making daily decisions for Adelaide's care. Lori hadn't warned me about how "knowing Adelaide best" was a double-edged sword: I didn't have a medical degree or fully comprehend the latest research, yet ultimately all decisions fell to me. That responsibility and ensuing pressure was inescapable.

Being at the hospital actually brought some relief. At least there, I didn't have to make emergency calls on my own; the burden was shared. Because at the end of the day, "have the fight" wasn't about fighting against her medical team (or competing against them . . .), but about fighting to be heard as a member of the team.

I SUPPOSE IT shouldn't have come as a shock when the hospital's in-house social worker began checking on us during our frequent inpatient stays. However, I was surprised to realize her concern was more for me than Adelaide.

"Do you have help at home?" she asked me.

"Not professional help. It's me and my husband, and I hire a nurse from the hospital to babysit a couple nights a month. I tried to apply for home nursing a couple months ago, but we were denied." What I didn't say was that because I wasn't working, I believed I should be able to take care of my daughter on my own.

"Caring for a child with Adelaide's conditions is incredibly challenging. If all your time is spent as her nurse, when do you get to be her mom?"

Well, shit.

Without realizing it, I had been spending so much time trying to keep Adelaide alive, analyzing every seizure and detailing every med change, that I was missing the joys of simply being her mother. During the moments when Adelaide was calm and content, I was racing around the house doing chores, answering emails, or taking advantage of the few moments where I could give Jackson my (nearly) undivided attention. Aside from bedtime, I rarely read to her anymore. Aside from seizures, I rarely sang to her. As much as I wanted to believe I could do it all, I couldn't.

"Let me help you reapply," she offered.

With the social worker's help, Adelaide qualified for twenty hours of in-home nursing care per week, in the form of two ten-hour shifts. However, due to nursing shortages, it ended up taking six months before we could even find a nurse to interview, and in the meantime, by the spring of 2018, Adelaide's seizures had reached a new level of nasty. Like clockwork, every morning she stared into space, her arm levitated, her body went stiff and then pulsed, her face turned red, and then her entire body lost tone. When she came to, she let out a blood-curdling scream before the entire sequence repeated itself over and over again. The cluster of seizures would build in intensity for five to ten minutes before finally easing off over another five minutes. All told, these seizures could last anywhere from eight to twenty excruciating minutes. We had an emergency medication we could administer rectally, but it knocked her out for hours afterward and caused her oxygen levels to drop, so we tried to hold off on giving it to her unless it was a particularly long-lasting seizure.

While the electrical storm raged in Adelaide's brain, there was nothing Miguel and I could do except take turns holding her and singing to her. At least that way, in the moments between the seizures, she knew she wasn't alone. We also held her hand, not out of comfort but so she wouldn't try to self-soothe by sucking her thumb only to bite down on her finger when the seizure returned. When it was over, we couldn't tell her that she was okay or that it would never happen again because we knew that it would happen again around the same time the next day.

Doctors and epilepsy patients alike have told me that it is unlikely the seizures themselves caused her physical pain, but that brought limited solace as it wasn't pain I saw on my daughter's face, but fear, helplessness, and confusion. No doubt a mirror of my own. After a month or so of adding and adjusting medications, Dr. Marcuccilli decided to bring her back to the hospital for more testing. We all agreed—there had to be something we were missing.

Dr. Marcuccilli entered our room early on a Wednesday morning. We'd come in the evening before and been welcomed by the nursing team and our favorite EEG technician, who had hooked Adelaide up to the familiar leads and wires.

"Good morning, Kelly," he said in my general direction while looking at Adelaide, who was now playing possum, feigning sleep in the hope that she would be left alone.

"Her EEG shows the hypsarrhythmia is back," Dr. Marcuccilli said, finally shifting his gaze to mine. He looked tired, his shoulders drooped.

My face fell into my hands, mirroring Adelaide's response. Hoping if I, too, played possum, evasion would alter reality. The infantile spasms had returned.

I don't know what I thought they would find. Maybe she had a new seizure type, maybe the seizures were coming from a different part of her brain . . . or more likely that there would be nothing conclusive, and we would be sent home to suffer through the seizures as we had so many times before.

"It's rare to see IS in a child over the age of two, but it can happen. We'll get her started on IV prednisolone in the hospital today, then you can take her home and monitor progress there."

Receiving this news was like being told a cancer in remission had returned. The steroid treatment wouldn't last as long as chemo, but it was still miserable. Her puffy face, uncomfortable bloated skin, the endless screaming of her 'roid rages. But there was no other option.

I let my hands drop from my face. Dr. Marcuccilli was patiently standing near Adelaide's bed, checking her vitals and the EEG leads on her head.

"Okay," was all I could say in response. We took Adelaide home.

SIX DAYS LATER, on a Monday morning, we were back on speaker phone with Dr. Marcuccilli. "So what do we do now?" Miguel asked him.

For a few days the prednisolone had worked, but then the screaming spasm/seizure clusters returned. This time, they were even more intense, lasted longer, and were happening multiple times a day.

We'd called Dr. Marcuccilli to beg for another solution.

"A combination of Acthar and Sabril," Dr. Marcuccilli responded.

If prednisolone was an obnoxious bully, then Acthar was a whole gang looking to fuck shit up. At least Sabril only had the side effect of very rarely leading to peripheral blindness. Aside from brain surgery, these are the only three known medications to treat infantile spasms. And because we didn't know what was causing Adelaide's seizures and couldn't identify where in the brain they were originating, surgery was not an option.

Desperate and out of options, we agreed to the plan, and Dr. Marcuccilli began the necessary paperwork to get these expensive drugs approved through our insurance. I assumed they would be approved just as they had been the last time Adelaide had taken them, when she was nine months old. I assumed we would have the drugs the next day because infantile spasms are a life-threatening emergency. But you know what they say about people who assume . . .

We filled out all the necessary paperwork and waited for insurance approval.

Then waited some more.

Then obsessively called Dr. Marcuccilli's office to ask for updates, but they hadn't heard anything either. We continued to wait while Adelaide continued to seize, and the hypsarrhythmia continued to damage her brain.

Finally, four days later, late afternoon on Friday, Dr. Marcuccilli called to let us know that our insurance had denied Acthar. According to their expertise as an insurance company, infantile spasms could only appear in children under the age of two, and therefore, the medication would be unnecessary. They recommended we try prednisolone. The same medication that had just failed to control Adelaide's spasms. Dr. Marcuccilli had requested a peer-to-peer review to challenge the decision, but going into the weekend there was nothing else we could do.

On Monday morning, I decided to reach out to the pharmaceutical company that made Acthar directly. The previous fall, I had been connected with representatives from Mallinckrodt Pharmaceuticals because they wanted to sponsor a fundraising campaign Miguel and I had spearheaded for CURE Epilepsy.

While the epilepsy community is grateful for Acthar, also commonly referred to as ACTH, we are less appreciative of the 97,000 percent price hike it has undergone over the years. Invented in the 1930s, Acthar had been on the market for $40 per vial before it was purchased in 2001 for $100,000 by a company called Questcor, which would, over time, raise the price of the life-saving drug to $36,000 a vial. Questcor claimed the price hike, one of the largest in American history, was out of necessity, as the company that owned the product before had been financially hemorrhaging. Facing legal trouble, Questcor was sold to Mallinckrodt in 2014. By 2018, Acthar cost $39,000 a vial, and Mallinckrodt would report net sales of *one billion dollars* for the medication.

I'd gone into the sponsorship discussion wary of accepting money from a company whose business model seemed questionable at best and downright moneygrubbing at worst. When their representatives failed to alter my gut impressions, using little more than deflection to defend Mallinckrodt's practices, we declined their assistance for our fundraiser. However, in their attempts to sway me, they had told me about a program the company provided that made sure any patient who needed the drug could receive it.

I may have turned down their money then, but with my daughter's life at stake, I wasn't above asking them for help now. Especially considering that, with Adelaide's current weight, her full course of treatment was going to require *five* vials of the medicine, bringing the grand total to $195,000. So Monday morning, I sent an email to my contact at Mallinckrodt.

Hi,

It has been a while, I hope you are both well. I am unfortunately writing because we are in a tough spot with our daughter, Adelaide. Her hypsarrhythmia has returned, and her epileptologist wants to put her back on high-dose ACTH. However, insurance has denied the ACTH because "she is over two years old." They obviously don't want to pay for the full treatment. We are appealing their decision, but Adelaide is declining and we need to do something now.

When we spoke last fall, you mentioned a program Mallinckrodt offered that provides patients ACTH even if their insurance denies the treatment. Can you please provide me with information on this program and what we need to do to get the ball rolling?

I appreciate your time and look forward to hearing back from you.

Best,
Kelly

I loathed pressing every key on my keyboard to write this email. I curdled knowing that the average family did not have the sort of influence apparently required to access support, and that as I typed this email there were no doubt other families also fighting to get this over-priced life-saving medication. I despised that I was again using connections to get Adelaide help, but most of all I was infuriated by the fact that I needed influence and connections at all to ensure her survival.

Their response came just twenty minutes later:

"Good morning, Kelly," the email began. My contact expressed sympathy that *"Adeline"* was once again battling hypsarrhythmia and that we were fighting with insurance. They directed me to send a denial of the referral letter to their Acthar Support and Access Program (currently renamed the "Acthar Patient Support and Reimbursement Program"), and said that I would *"be in great hands"* and to keep them posted on *"Adeline's"* progress.

Her name is Adelaide, assholes.

Their quick response had given me hope . . . until I learned that the Acthar Support and Access Program was outsourced to another company entirely. I prepared myself for what I feared would be a drawn-out bureaucratic process, insensitive to the patient and family in crisis.

The rest of the day was spent on the phone providing all the information the patient access program required to process the request and get us set up with the specialty pharmacy. Everything seemed to be on track, and I hoped we would have the medicine by Wednesday. I was so confident that I told Dr. Marcuccilli that he could stop fighting with our insurance and get back to his other patients.

Big mistake. Huge.

On Tuesday, the case manager called to inform me that we were being denied the financial assistance because our annual income was above their cutoff.

"To be clear, my daughter needs five vials totaling $195,000, and unless my family makes under $175,000 a year, which is $20,000 less than the total cost of the medication, we don't qualify for assistance?" I asked the outsourced case manager.

"That's correct," she said apologetically.

"You know that's ridiculous, right?"

"You can write a letter of appeal that includes all of your family's medical expenses," she offered, growing increasingly uncomfortable.

"Can you transfer me to someone at Mallinckrodt?" I asked.

"I'm sorry, but I don't have access to anyone at Mallinckrodt. We're a separate company."

I wanted to scream, to slam my phone down like a classic landline hang-up. I wanted to throw my hands up in the air and say I did everything I could and give up. I wanted to crawl under the covers and sob. I wanted to run away.

But then Adelaide started screaming, and I turned to find her mid-seizure. So instead I just hung up.

"It's going to be okay, sweet girl. Mommy's here. I love you." I held her, swaying back and forth. I watched for when the light came back to her eyes, so I'd know to grip her hand to prevent her from biting her thumb when the seizure returned. Then released it when the light faded so that I didn't injure her arm when she went stiff and shook.

For twenty minutes we repeated the cycle until, with no end to the seizure cluster in sight, I delivered the rectal medicine and connected her to the oxygen I knew she would require.

I was too tired to cry, too angry to think straight. I rage-dreamed of inviting the pharmaceutical and insurance gatekeepers to our home to witness the epileptic hell Adelaide and our family endured daily. I wanted to force them to hold her and listen to her scream. How dare anyone prevent me from accessing the *only* medication left that could help her.

When Adelaide was stable and sleeping off the seizure and the medication's side effects, I called my "friends" at Mallinckrodt. I described Adelaide's seizures in vivid detail and told them about the ludicrous financial threshold that they should have known about. I reminded them that they had promised me the drug was available to everyone who needed it. And then I might have insinuated that if we didn't get the medication soon, others would find out.

I almost didn't recognize myself. This wasn't me: I didn't throw around thinly veiled threats about going public with a story to get what I wanted. I wasn't the person who used my family's influence to get what I needed. Except I was, and this wasn't even the first time.

Until you are fully enmeshed in the American medical system, either as an employee or a patient or caregiver, I don't think you can truly understand how secondary providing care to patients is to the business model. In theory, I understood these were all for-profit companies, but the reality of what that meant was still chilling. My sick child was lucky enough to be born into a family with means and influence, not to mention white skin and the ability to speak English. It was only with these privileges that we had a real chance to get Adelaide the care she needed—as long as I sacrificed my integrity along the way.

By Wednesday morning, Mallinckrodt had sent a waiver to the Support and Access Program overriding the income threshold for our case, but for some reason I still had to write the personal appeal and include the list of our annual medical expenses. So while Adelaide received an immunoglobulin infusion to treat her mast cell activation syndrome, I sat in the hospital's infusion clinic going back and forth with a Mallinckrodt rep and Adelaide's case manager, filling out even more paperwork from my phone.

After three days of relentless emails and calls to get all the paperwork they required, I was told that Mallinckrodt now needed to hear from Adelaide's doctor to confirm the order for the script he had already written.

In between seeing all his other patients, Dr. Marcuccilli played his own game of phone tag with the Support and Access Program. It wasn't until Thursday afternoon, after he had connected with them three separate times, that they took down the order correctly. As frustrated as I was, it was encouraging to know that I wasn't fighting alone. We were a team; I couldn't have done this without Dr. Marcuccilli's dedication.

ON FRIDAY MORNING—*SEVENTEEN days* after we sought treatment for Adelaide's intensifying seizures—I received confirmation that the medication had shipped and would be received that day. I've never felt more relieved injecting my daughter's thigh with a medication I knew would turn her into a rage-fueled monster. We never received a bill for the medication. Maybe they finally got our insurance to cover it. I never asked.

How much additional damage had been done to Adelaide's brain in the week we waited for insurance approval? And in the following week, in which we'd bent over backward for Mallinckrodt, providing everything short of a kidney for their files? How much longer would we have had to wait if Miguel wasn't Hamilton? How much more time would Dr. Marcuccilli have had to spend, away from his other patients, fighting with our insurance company or Mallinckrodt? How do you expect someone to pay nearly $200,000 for one life-saving treatment of a medication that has existed since the 1930s?!

But all these questions assume that our medical system is broken. The real problem is that it is functioning exactly as it was designed. From the medical institutions and pharmaceutical companies that see my daughter as a cash cow to the insurance companies who see her as a liability.

Have the fight.

I wanted to shout all of this into a reporter's microphone, to raise alarms and fight for systemic changes in hopes of preventing this from happening to another child and their family. But I was terrified that Adelaide would need the treatment again and that, if I pissed off the makers of the drug, we wouldn't be able to get it the next time. Instead,

I held my nose and tongue while shamefully accepting the vials valued at more than four hundred times their volume in pure gold.

Once Adelaide was tolerating the Acthar, we added the Sabril a week later. The combination of the two medications eliminated the disastrous brain wave pattern, hypsarrhythmia. The number, length, and intensity of her seizures decreased dramatically as well. We will never know whether the damage done was inevitable or exacerbated by the delay in treatment. What I do know is that we never saw Adelaide laugh or smile again.

CHAPTER SIXTEEN
The Partner

The wounds left by my college relationship were healed through the love and trust of my relationship with Miguel. The wounds left by losing Elvis and nearly losing Adelaide were blossoming into advocacy and necessary resilience. But there were other gaping wounds I had suppressed so deeply that I nearly forgot they existed. However, no emotional depth is unreachable, especially when met by just the right image, sound, or smell. Which was how a decade-old trauma found its way back to me.

Miguel was at the theater, Jackson was on the couch with his iPad, and Adelaide was in her bedroom with Alison, the home nurse we'd finally found. I prepared dinner with Tabasco circling my feet in hopes I'd accidentally drop a chunk of chicken. The news played on the TV in the background.

"*In the wake of the Harvey Weinstein scandal . . .*" My heart rate quickened, and I reached to change the channel. These recent sexual assault reports were affecting me in ways I didn't understand. "*. . . new* *allegations against a famous movie director. The* Los Angeles Times *reports that James Toback has been accused of sexually harassing more than thirty women over the last three decades . . ."*

The blood drained from my face. Staring back at me from the TV screen were Toback's beady eyes. I needed to run, to hide. Without a word, I turned from the kitchen and quickly walked to Miguel's and my bedroom, but once there I still felt too exposed. I moved to the bathroom, turning off the lights and closing the door behind me.

Huddled on the floor of our bathroom, eleven years of repressed memories resurfaced: being stopped on the street, the restaurant, his "office." As if I was twenty-four again, the shame of the events settled on me like a thick, sticky residue. I startled when Tabasco pawed on the door, begging to be let into the bathroom, my shadow always needing to be near me.

Alone later that night, after I had served and cleared dinner and put both kids to bed, I scoured Twitter and news articles for any information I could find. What I discovered shocked me: I was one of likely hundreds of women that Toback had similarly assaulted over the decades. The details of our stories were hauntingly similar. Knowing that I wasn't the only one brought a twisted solace. For once, I was glad that I wasn't special.

Whether it was because I was older now or that the public discourse around "the casting couch" had shifted, I now understood that this shame was not mine to bear. To rinse it off, I resolved to share what had happened, and I started with Miguel.

I waited until Jackson was at school and approached Miguel while he was sitting on the couch with his phone and coffee. Nurse Alison was off that day, and Adelaide was resting in her chair, her feeding pump delivering a liquid breakfast through her G-tube and into her stomach. Tabasco jumped up on the couch and nestled next to me.

As I recounted the uncomfortable details, my skin crawled with disgust. In Miguel's eyes, I saw discomfort turn to rage, which dissolved into pain and concern, and I recognized that, as difficult as it was for me to share, it was also incredibly difficult for Miguel to hear.

"I remember you telling me you were meeting up with him, and then you never talked about it again. I knew something hadn't been right."

Miguel pulled me close before adding, "I love you, and I'm sorry that happened. I wish I had been there."

"I don't know that it would have made a difference."

"Why didn't you tell me?" he asked, compassion in his voice.

"I was twenty-four, and I worried you would think I had cheated on you," I said. "I also thought it was my fault because I allowed it to happen. And then I guess I repressed the memory, which wasn't something I realized you could do as an adult. But now I know better—I know it wasn't my fault."

Miguel hugged me again. "What a fucking creep. Can you report him?"

"I can try." Even if nothing came of it, there was something to be said about owning the narrative. Then maybe I could reclaim the power that Toback had taken from me that early fall night.

Empowered by Miguel's support, I shared my story with investigators in New York and Los Angeles. Unfortunately, even with the number of women coming forward, the statute of limitations had expired and there was little that could be done legally. There may not have been justice within the court system (yet), but Toback hasn't formally worked in Hollywood since 2017. My stomach still turns when I think of him, but with the shame cleared away another wound has air to heal.

I HAD CERTAINLY grown since my ingenue years, and so had Miguel. Being a father had brought out the best in him, as I'd known it would. When I was ready to lose my mind because a sloth could get ready for school faster than Jackson, Miguel managed to keep his cool and get him out the door. When I accidentally pulled Adelaide's G-tube out of her stomach, Miguel watched a YouTube video on how to replace it, avoiding an ER visit. We weren't just growing independently; we were growing together.

With Miguel, I didn't have to explain how helpless I felt holding Adelaide through a seizure, or the desperation that came when another medication failed her. The growing lines on his face told me he felt it too. We needed each other to feel sane, seen, and less alone.

Though it had taken months, we had eventually found an evolving balance in our home. With the help of the ever-updating medication schedule on the fridge, Miguel took over care for Adelaide when I left home. And even if Miguel couldn't attend all of Adelaide's doctor appointments with me, he was aware of her test results, treatments, and the latest theories, so he remained involved in the major medical decisions. We continued to find systems that worked for us, until they didn't, and then we came up with new systems. Which I suppose is not so different from typical parenting; it's just that our stakes were unusually high.

While our new normal was anything but, I still sought out moments of our old life. On Saturdays, if Adelaide was relatively stable, I would load the kids into the car and drive twenty minutes to the theater to have dinner with Miguel in between his matinee and evening performances—just as I had done with Jackson when he was Adelaide's age. Not only did it give Miguel time with the kids, but it also offered me a small break and change of scenery.

I always made sure to look extra cute for these visits. I joked that I needed to scare off the other women in the building. But I wasn't really joking. I was abundantly aware of how stressful our life was at home, and how Miguel was able to escape each day to a job where he was surrounded by beautiful, talented women—and that he had a private dressing room. Miguel had never given me any reason not to trust him, but being financially dependent on someone else for the first time in my adult life, while entrenched in the stress of medical caregiving, left me feeling vulnerable and ill-prepared. It was likely also the result of some lingering Ryan-era insecurities. But also have you seen professional dancers? They're stunning!

"If you cheat on me, I will take you for everything you are worth," I would remind him with varying amounts of levity. Honestly, I didn't know what I would do, but I figured it didn't hurt to establish what was at risk.

"Why would I ruin everything we have for that? There's no world where it would be worth it," Miguel responded each time. I was as grateful for his reassurances as I was for his patience.

The few friends I knew who had gotten divorces admitted that when they separated, it had been months, if not years, since they and their spouse had had sex. We were only a few years removed from losing Elvis, and I hadn't forgotten the pain Miguel felt when I'd shuddered at his touch. In the years since, we had learned to communicate more openly and regularly. All things considered, our relationship felt as stable as it ever had. Still, I was anxiously aware that marriages had crumbled under far less.

So sex night, a weekly scheduled event, was born. This was real sex, no quickies allowed. Even if I was exhausted, I powered through because no matter how tired I was, I never regretted the intimacy the following morning. Also, not for nothing, it was fun and felt great. Twenty-something me would have been appalled at the lack of spontaneity and romance. But thirty-something me knew that our clothing-optional days of staying in bed and having bagels delivered at noon were behind us.

Beep beep beep . . . beep beep. Beep beep beep . . . beep beep.

"Come on, Adelaide!" I whispered into the dark. The pulse oximeter alarm was alerting us to a drop in Adelaide's oxygen levels. This now occurred so frequently that our initial sharp fears of the alarm had dulled.

Tonight, however, there was an added layer of annoyance. It was sex night, and her timing was exceptionally poor.

"Maybe she'll recover on her own," Miguel said, coming up from under the covers. We froze, listening, waiting.

Beep beep beep . . . beep beep. Beep beep beep . . . beep beep.

I sighed, pulling myself away from the warmth of Miguel's body and back to our medically complex reality. Miguel looked at me longingly as I pulled on a robe. For a moment I was carried back to our wedding, dancing to "The Luckiest" and gazing at the firework-strewn sky.

When my eyes had adjusted from the dark hall to the low light in Adelaide's room, the cause of the alarm was evident. In an attempt to suck her thumb, Adelaide had hooked the nasal cannula supplying her additional oxygen and pulled it from her nose. I repositioned her and taped the cannula back into place.

"Adelaidey aidey baby, Adelaide aidey baby, Adelaide, Adelaide, Adelaidey Grace," I sang while running my fingers through her hair until I saw her heart rate come down and her oxygen levels stabilize.

Adelaide erratically sucked her thumb every few moments whenever she stirred enough to remember it was there. She was even more beautiful now than the first day I'd held her. I knew other people first saw the oxygen cannula taped to her cheeks, the tip of her tongue protruding from her tiny mouth, her physical weakness. What they missed was her vibrant personality, feistiness, and determination to live. Adelaide had ample opportunities to give up, but instead she chose to keep going. Even if that meant sabotaging her oxygen intake for a more comfortable thumb-sucking position.

"Is she okay?" Miguel asked as I shed my robe and climbed back into bed.

"For now," I answered, letting him kiss my mouth, neck, and chest.

For a moment, I was tempted to ask him if he thought we were or ever would be "the luckiest" again. But in that moment, under the covers, our children once again safely sleeping in their beds, I decided for myself that no matter what, we were lucky to have each other.

While the sex was great, our conversations afterward were equally intimate and binding. Engulfed in the dark, there was an unvoiced, judgment-free understanding. And if a reactive face *was* made, it couldn't be seen anyway. It also helped that during these conversations, my always on-the-go husband was seemingly held captive by our sheets.

"Do you ever feel like we are missing out on fully enjoying life's highs because we are always so worried about Adelaide?" I asked the shadows that night.

"I used to," he answered. "*Hamilton* was this rocket, and who knew where it would take us next. And Adelaide, or her medical stuff, was the parachute holding us back. But maybe those things are actually grounding us, reminding us what is most important. Allowing us to appreciate the highs that much more."

"Huh, I like that."

What I couldn't reconcile was the physical cost of this extra meaning for Adelaide, and the mental bill the rest of us were footing. Nothing could ever make up for that. I rolled over in hopes that a physical repositioning, like the tilt of an Etch A Sketch, would quiet and reset my brain. Then, just as sleep was tempting me—

Beep beep beep . . . beep beep. Beep beep beep . . . beep beep.

Miguel was lightly snoring beside me. How her alarms rarely woke him was all at once infuriating and fascinating. However, even in that moment of spousal annoyance, I knew I would do everything in my power to protect our marriage. Tonight was no exception; it was just going to require that I do it down the hall. With my pillow in hand, I again made the short walk to Adelaide's room.

On the outside, I was putting on a strong face—because I *was* strong, but also because I feared if I thought too much about the circumstances of our day-to-day life, I would fall apart, and I wasn't sure I'd be able to put myself back together again afterward. The social worker at the hospital back when Adelaide's seizures worsened had been right: I needed help.

Nurse Alison was wonderful—and a huge improvement from the first nurse I hired, who never returned after her first training shift, citing that she was overwhelmed by the level of care Adelaide required. *Really, lady?* To quote King George in *Hamilton*, "I wasn't aware that was something a person could do."

It had taken the hospital's social worker nudging our home nursing company, but eventually they sent Alison. She walked into our home that first day, and every day after, with a quiet but assertive energy. She looked to be in her mid-to-late twenties with long blonde hair she pulled back in a pony tail and blue eyes she often hid behind glasses. But there was something about her that told me she understood a lot more about life than I had when I was twenty-something, running between auditions and serving disco fries. During her first visit, I asked her if she would like to hold Adelaide—what had become my litmus test.

"I would love to," she answered.

Alison took Adelaide with ease, which was saying something, considering Adelaide now weighed nearly thirty pounds. Not to mention how her lack of muscle tone left you feeling like you were supporting a very cute sack of potatoes. Sensing a new person, Adelaide closed her eyes in Alison's arms.

"Are you hiding from me?" Alison asked Adelaide, smiling.

"She has a tendency to play possum with new people, or basically anyone in a white doctor's coat," I answered for her.

"That's okay. You open your eyes whenever you're ready," she told Adelaide.

I hadn't been sure how I would feel having a stranger in our home taking care of my daughter, but Alison's calm and assertive energy put us all at ease. The two shifts a week Adelaide qualified for quickly felt paltry and insufficient. Fortunately, after several weeks, and as a direct result of Alison's detailed notes, we were able to get additional nursing hours approved. By the end of the summer, Alison was with us for four ten-hour shifts per week, and I was also interviewing night nurses to help a couple nights a week. I couldn't remember the last time I had slept for longer than a two-hour stretch.

Having Alison in our home at regularly scheduled times gave me a tentative freedom I hadn't felt in two years. I got more involved with CURE Epilepsy, started writing a blog, and planned weekly dinner dates with Jackson at a restaurant down the street from our apartment. Most importantly, though, it allowed me to enjoy being Adelaide's mother.

There is a difference between being a caregiver and being a parent. Being a caregiver is a (often unpaid) job. Being a parent, on the other hand, is a relationship. Now, the responsibilities of that relationship can include caregiving, but the degrees vary. While Alison prepared medications, Adelaide and I snuggled, read books, or played with her therapy toys. With my caregiving responsibilities lessened, I could direct my energy toward the nurturing aspects of motherhood.

Alison was more than just a respite. She became our partner in Adelaide's care, another advocate in Adelaide's corner. She helped me analyze Adelaide's improvements and regressions as well as determine when it was time for Adelaide to be readmitted to the hospital. While Alison tried very hard to keep her relationship with our family professional, it wasn't hard to see how much she cared for Adelaide emotionally.

Returning home after a CURE Epilepsy meeting one warm summer afternoon, I was welcomed by the velvety tones of Frank Sinatra playing on our living room speaker. Adelaide was propped up in her adaptive chair, bright-eyed and tracking me across the room, while Alison prepared her lunch.

"Hi! I hope it's okay that I play music." Alison said.

"Of course it is. Are you a Sinatra fan?" I asked.

"Who isn't? But it turns out so is Adelaide."

I smiled, a little in disbelief and perhaps also a little jealous that Alison knew something about my daughter that I didn't.

"I was surfing through music to play for her and started with some Baby Einstein. She stayed in possum mode, no reaction. Then, I tried 'Baby Shark,' and oh, did I get a reaction: a scream followed by leg kicks. She was *not* having it."

I laughed at the image, noting Alison's appreciation for my girl's sass.

"I switched to a jazz station, and the fussing and kicking stopped, then Frank Sinatra came on—'Fly Me to the Moon.' Her eyes opened wide, zero fussing, totally relaxed. She's been alert and awake since."

Whether Alison knew it or not, in that moment she could have asked for anything in the world and I would have bartered, clawed, and fought to get it for her. She had given me new insight into my daughter. Professional boundaries be damned: she was family now.

Having Nurse Alison working in our home on weekdays also gave me the energy to spend more time at events with Miguel on his evenings off—energy I could not have gone without during the gauntlet that awaited us in the last two weeks of October 2018.

On October 14th, we threw Adelaide's third birthday party. I was so thrilled we had survived another year and was keenly aware that additional years were not guaranteed. Naturally, I went all out. I invited more people to the party than came to our wedding. I remember it as a bright afternoon spent celebrating our daughter with friends. The reality was more complicated. She had just come off her ketogenic diet and was allowed to have her first taste of frosting—like ever, in her life. But only minutes after the smallest taste, she had a seizure. We all acted normal about it because, to us, it was. To anyone on the outside, though, our normal was about as typical as repetitive shark attacks.

That evening, in front of many of the same family and friends, Miguel and I were honored at an event for our commitment to the epilepsy community.

"I want to take a moment to acknowledge the true star of the Cervantes family," Miguel said when it was time for us to speak. "I get up on stage each night, talk real fast, and move my hands around a lot, and everyone gives me a standing ovation. But at home, Kelly is Adelaide's primary caregiver, managing it all. No one gives the caregivers standing ovations, but I think they should." And then Miguel handed me the microphone and started to applaud, the rest of the room joining him.

My nose itched as I fought back tears. "Thank you," I mouthed to Miguel.

For so long, I had craved this recognition for doing my job and doing it well—just as anyone else might wish for acknowledgment in their career. Okay, so most people don't get standing ovations, but they might get a raise, or even a gracious email. Those things don't happen when your job is medically caring for a family member. Caregiving is just something you are expected to do and is often met with pity over admiration.

Of course I knew that Miguel was grateful for the additional weight I had been carrying since our familial restructuring. He had told me as much. But hearing it said out loud in front of friends, family, and strangers alike reinforced that value and healed a bit of my damaged ego.

As if that wasn't enough excitement for an entire month, the next day was CURE Epilepsy's annual benefit where I spoke in front of over a thousand people, and Miguel performed alongside the event's headliners, Rock and Roll Hall of Famers Eddie Vedder and Nils Lofgren. From cupcakes and seizures to ovations and rock stars, who were we and what was this life?

There was no denying that the magic of the weekend had been created by Adelaide. Sure, without *Hamilton* we wouldn't even be in Chicago, and Miguel certainly would not have been asked to perform with rock legends. But it was because of Adelaide that we were connected to CURE Epilepsy and our incredible community of friends. It was because of Adelaide we had found this extended purpose. Perhaps we had it backward. Perhaps Adelaide had been the rocket all along.

We were brought back down to Earth two days later, on Adelaide's actual birthday, when we rushed her to the hospital with increased seizures and high carbon dioxide levels. *Hamilton* Shmamilton, Adelaide was her own rocket *and* parachute. After three nights in the pediatric intensive care unit with no answers, we were released. The rest of that week we went to a Chicago Blackhawks hockey game (with Jackson and Adelaide), I spoke at a benefit for the ACLU of Illinois on the importance of a woman's right to choose (love you, Elvis), attended a pre-Halloween party (with Miguel and I as your favorite childhood globe-trotters, Carmen Sandiego and Where's Waldo), before closing out the week on the sideline of a Chicago Bears football game.

I never could have dreamed of attending even one of these events without Adelaide's incredible army of home nurses and nurse babysitters. Because I could trust them in my absence, Miguel and I were able to enjoy the perks of his Chicago stardom while he had it. My mom guilt was still as thick as a slice of deep-dish pizza, but the stress of Adelaide's health was going to be there whether we got to meet NFL quarterbacks or not. And as Miguel liked to say, "People aren't going to care about me being Hamilton forever, so we might as well enjoy it while it lasts!"

My phone was always in my hand, and I was ready to bolt home at the first sign of concern. But I also knew Adelaide was in very capable hands. These events and date nights were important both in the moment and as memories. Miguel and I may have been strapped into one of the world's wildest roller coasters, but we were strapped into it together: clinging to the safety bar for dear life one moment and screaming joyfully the next.

The day after the football game, less than ten days since our previous hospital stay, we were back in the PICU. Adelaide spent Halloween day dressed as Wonder Woman before changing into a ladybug costume for evening rounds. I left my Adelaideybug in the hospital to take Jackson, dressed as a rock star, trick or treating with friends in our neighborhood. Eventually, I brought him back to the hospital where he cleaned the nurses out of their candy stash and cuddled with his sister in her hospital bed until his daddy could pick him up after work.

"Hey, sexy wife," Miguel said, answering my phone call the following morning.

"We're being discharged this afternoon!" I told him.

"Alright! I don't have to be at the theater until this evening, so just let me know when I should pick you up." We both knew it was only a matter of time before we would have to rush Adelaide back to the hospital, but hopefully this time it would be months, not weeks or days.

"I love you," I told him before hanging up.

"I love you too."

This wasn't the marriage I had envisioned as a self-conscious teen learning lessons from *90210* or as the insecure girlfriend sabotaging dreams for imagined security. Well, maybe I'd imagined the glamorous-rock-star days—but certainly not the braless-in-my-daughter's-hospital-room days. I didn't dare imagine what my future looked like now, but facing Adelaide's worst moments with Miguel gave me hope that whatever lay ahead, we would survive it together.

CHAPTER SEVENTEEN
The Unready

Christmas had been a veritable disaster. Wanting a break from the city, I agreed to travel with the kids to my parents, who had retired and left Omaha for North Carolina, on my own. Miguel would join us on Christmas Eve and head back to work on the 26th.

"You guys look like a small traveling rock band," Dad commented when he picked us up from the airport. Adelaide was now using a ventilator at night, in addition to the oxygen. But you can't take a flammable oxygen tank on an airplane, so we also traveled with a portable oxygen concentrator. Additionally, we had her medical-grade food and the feeding pump through which she received it, all her medications, and a duffel bag full of supplies similar to an EMT's.

I was determined, though, to lead as normal a life as possible—or try, anyway. That included going to Grandma and Grandpa's for Christmas. If I was the tour manager, six-year-old Jackson was our roadie, helping me with the luggage, and Adelaide was the pampered star. A star who decided to keep our tour exciting.

"What do you mean you resuscitated her last night?" Mom asked Christmas Eve morning.

"Her alarms went off, but readjusting her and upping the oxygen didn't work, so I used the Ambu bag Alison packed for emergencies and got her breathing again," I answered, taking a sip of my coffee. *Dad makes it weaker than we do at home. I'll need to make another pot.*

"If it happens again tonight, come and get me. You shouldn't do that alone."

"Her alarms go off all the time; I'm used to stabilizing her."

"I know, but not with an Ambu bag, Kelly. That's scary. Promise you'll come and get me."

I didn't want to admit how scared I was because I didn't want to acknowledge how close Adelaide's brushes with the other side were getting. When her alarms went off again that night, and again none of my usual interventions worked, I kept my promise and ran to my parents' bedroom. Mom, having heard the alarms, was already closing the door behind her. Together, we made sure Adelaide survived another night. And thank goodness, because that would have made for an exceptionally shitty Christmas morning.

"CAN YOU REMEMBER the last month when Adelaide was doing better than the previous month?" I asked Miguel when we were back home in Chicago after the holidays.

He thought about it for a moment. "August? Maybe September?"

"Yeah . . ." That made it at least four straight months of decline.

The severity of her seizures had lessened after the battle to get the most recent round of ACTH and Sabril, but her overall health— respiratory function, heart rate, and MCAS symptoms—were worse than ever. Additionally, her eyes, when she opened them, were only slits, and perhaps most heartbreakingly, she was having a hard time sucking her thumb—her only way to self-soothe. She would try so hard to get that thumb into her mouth but couldn't manage the coordination. Stubborn like her mommy, she would get angry and pull away from my guiding hand as if saying, *I can do it myself!* But she couldn't, not anymore.

Up to this point, we had always been able to pinpoint a reason for her regressions, whether it was seizures, mast cell activation, or a bad setting change on her ventilator. Was the hypsarrhythmia back? Were there seizures occurring deep in her brain that weren't visible on the surface? Or was this a word that had haunted us since our earliest days: neurodegeneration?

"Could you imagine anything worse than if she has some sort of neurodegenerative condition that she dies from slowly until she's like four years old?" I had asked Mom years ago when we had first started this diagnostic odyssey.

"No, I can't. But so far, she's been negative for all known neurodegenerative genetic conditions, right?"

"Yeah . . . so far."

Miguel adamantly believed that one of the drugs she was taking, or a combination thereof, was causing the continued regression. Meanwhile, I was terrified that if we took her off the wrong medication, we would be letting the infantile spasms genie out of its bottle and be unable to regain control.

But now I could hear the word whispered around me again. Her doctors were running out of other explanations and had ordered another MRI to compare to one from several months earlier.

"Is Adelaide's dad able to join us at 3 PM tomorrow afternoon? We are scheduling a meeting with her entire care team to discuss next steps," the PICU pediatrician asked during our latest hospital admission.

Her entire team in one room. This was a first.

Miguel was able to join, and we entered the conference room together. The harsh fluorescent lighting emphasized the room's sterility. A large table that could seat at least sixteen people took up most of the space. There were no windows, no art on the white walls. It felt like a cartoon image of purgatory you might see in *The New Yorker*, where spirits are waiting to see whether they will be entering heaven or hell.

Miguel and I took seats near the door next to the social worker that had helped us apply for nursing the year before. Eventually, Dr. Marcuccilli (retro doctor bag in hand), Adelaide's mast cell doctor Dr. Talbot, her sleep doctor, and the PICU pediatrician all took seats around the massive table. There were a few other faces that I recognized: the hospital pharmacist, a PICU nurse, and an assistant or two. Her pulmonologist, cardiologist, and gastroenterologist were notably missing.

The PICU pediatrician started by giving an update on Adelaide's current admission, then each doctor added their own assessment. Dr. Marcuccilli went last. He pulled a single sheet of paper from a file folder.

"We received the results back from Adelaide's most recent brain MRI, and I've compared it with the one she had four months ago. Her brain has lost volume, which is a trend we have also seen in her last three MRIs. At first, I thought this could be a result of her increased steroid use, but it has been months since she was last on steroids, and yet her brain continues to get smaller." Dr. Marcuccilli was hunched over the papers on the table, head bowed, shoulders slumped.

He hadn't yet said the word, but given his audience, he didn't need to. This was conclusive evidence of neurodegeneration.

My baby girl's brain was dying.

Adelaide was dying.

My own brain, either out of solidarity or trauma, stopped processing the information around me. I was crying, and someone gave me a tissue. Miguel asked questions and someone answered. Condolences were offered, and then everyone left. The specifics are lost to me. Like waking from a nightmare, I remember the feelings but not the details.

When the room had emptied, Miguel stood first and offered me his hand. Right now, our daughter was still alive in a hospital bed down the hall, and she needed us. We walked out the door and into hell together.

EVEN THOUGH WE had confirmation that Adelaide's condition was neurodegenerative, and there was nothing the doctors could do to stop it, no one could tell us how long she had left. The best guesses were somewhere between several months to a couple years. With no evidence to back me up, other than sheer force of will, I chose to believe we had years.

Our priorities for Adelaide's care shifted from treatment and symptom improvement to quality of life and comfort. It was much easier to keep her comfortable in our home, so Jenny and her kids started coming to us on Friday nights. During what we dubbed FNL, or Friday Night Laughs, we watched questionably appropriate stand-up specials over takeout and margaritas with Adelaide sandwiched between us on the couch.

"I've got the margs, you order the pizza." Jenny instructed, stopping to greet Tabasco as she walked into our apartment. "Basky! Who's a good boy?"

"Would you like Adelaide in her bedroom or out here in the family room with you?" Alison asked.

"Oh, she needs to be out here with us," Jenny answered. "She needs her shuggies."

"Out here is fine, thank you," I said.

Alison gathered her belongings and began to put on her jacket.

"Wait, you can't leave without your margarita!" Jenny called to her.

"Thank you, but you know I can't take that," Alison answered.

"Why not! It's Friday, save it for when you get home!" Jenny pushed.

"Have a good weekend, Kelly, I'll see you on Monday." Alison smiled and snuck out the door.

"You know she is never going to take a drink from you, right?" I said, pulling up the number to the pizza place on my phone. Jenny had been trying for weeks now, but Alison was nothing if not diligent and appropriate.

"She should; they're delicious."

JUST AS ADELAIDE's epilepsy and *Hamilton* had come into our lives during the same week, their exit was announced in tandem as well. The Chicago production of *Hamilton* would close on January 5, 2020. Under any other circumstance, our conversations at home would have been filled with questions, ideas, and plans for the future: Would we stay in Chicago so we could be close to Adelaide's medical team? Move back east where there was a better chance of Miguel getting another job that allowed us to keep our health insurance? Throw our hands in the air and run off to Costa Rica? But I was done making plans for a future that was deaf to my pleas, prayers, and screams.

Instead, we did our best to live in the moment, and there was no better place to do that than Lake Michigan. For three summers, we had been fortunate to rent a beautiful cottage on Lake Michigan, where we invited friends and family to join us for a week or two of detached bliss. The first year, our matchmaker Jeff and his family had stayed with us; the following year, Miguel's best friend from his *Spelling Bee* days, Eric, had come with his family. This year we would spend a week with Miguel's family and a week with mine.

Cell phones were exchanged for books, and video games for sand buckets. The small community in Michigan was only two and a half hours from Chicago and the same one I had been visiting since I was a small child. Having moved around so much in my life, this was one of the few touchpoints I could return to. The wooden cottages, tree-lined paths, shifting dunes, and shimmering lake—it was all a time capsule. Every alcove and bench was touched by a memory: building drip sandcastles with my Mimi, feeding ducks off a dock with Dad, walking out to the Big Red Lighthouse after a storm to see what had washed ashore. And now I got to repeat it all with my own children.

In Michigan, Adelaide also seemed to relax. Maybe it was because she wasn't being carried in and out of the car to appointments, because life was slower here, or because she was surrounded by family. I almost want to say she even had fewer seizures in Michigan, but I'm not sure that's true. What's more likely is that the sound of the waves on the beach dulled the sharp edges of the trauma that accompanied them.

Alison was able to join us for the last few days of the vacation, allowing me true moments of respite. Prior to her arrival, I chose to stay with Adelaide on the deck of the beach house. The thought of bringing Adelaide and her equipment down the beach was too daunting a task. But on our final day, Alison helped me prepare everything Adelaide would need and we carried it out to a small tent on the beach. Finally, it was Miss A's turn. Once she was all decked out in an adorable blue and white floral bikini with matching sunglasses, Miguel carried her to the beach to join us. Mig, Jackson, Alison, and I all took turns sitting with her in the tiny tent. We let her feel the sand beneath her toes, read her stories, and sat quietly listening to the waves. She was so calm, so content. Sitting on the beach that day, she was healthier and more stable than she had been in months: no seizures, no oxygen desaturations, no heart rate spikes or drops. I yearned for the Earth to stay still so we could live in this day forever. But the sun persisted in its relentless track across the sky, and all too soon it was time to head back to the cottage to rinse off the day and prepare for the trip home.

THE BENEFITS OF the Michigan air would not carry back to Chicago. Adelaide's decline was sharp and undeniable. Her body stopped tolerating some of her treatments, and she would cry for hours with no obvious source for her pain or discomfort. Alison and I took turns rocking her in her bedroom to soothe her, as she was unable to suck her thumb and had no other way to soothe herself.

We hadn't yet been back for a week when Alison brought it up. "Kelly," she started cautiously, "I think it's time to consider hospice." She was sitting in the rocking chair, catching up on the day's medical notes, while I kneeled next to a finally resting Adelaide.

"I'm not ready," I said, never looking up from my daughter.

"This is hard, but it's not up to you and when you're ready. Adelaide is struggling. We can't make her better, but we *can* bring her comfort. Hospice can bring her comfort." She was as calm as ever, but I could hear the pleading in her voice. I knew she loved Adelaide. I could see it in the way she said goodbye to her each evening, letting Adelaide know how proud she was of her, telling her when she would be back to see her, and then kissing her own fingers and touching them to Adelaide's forehead. I knew she wanted what was best for Adelaide. I knew all of this, and yet . . .

"I'm not ready." I got up and left the room.

I had been fighting for Adelaide's life for nearly four years. From the days of weighing her on a fruit scale to trekking all over the country trying to find someone with answers. In addition to being her mother, being her caregiver and advocate had become my identity. How was I supposed to know when to let go? And how could anyone expect me to let go at all?

Alison wasn't the only person trying to talk to me about end-of-life care. There were the nurses and doctors in the hospital who kept asking me if I had signed a do not resuscitate form, otherwise known as a DNR. I wanted to scream at them: *No, assholes, I want you to save her. It's your fucking job to save her.* How could they even ask me that?

Then there was the social worker from the palliative care company we had brought on following Adelaide's neurodegenerative diagnosis. She explained that a hospice team would support our family by simplifying Adelaide's care for us. They would take over supplying all of Adelaide's food, medical supplies, and care items. They would visit us at least once a week, supply pain medications, and be a compassionate source of information as Miguel and I continued to make challenging decisions regarding her care and beyond.

And beyond.

I couldn't believe that once more, I was being asked to decide when to end our child's life. Of course, this time I wouldn't run the risk of being chastised the way I had been after making this decision for Elvis. This time I would be met with compassion and sympathy, even though the only difference was that Elvis had been inside my body while Adelaide was outside.

We have a lot of work to do, little girl.

Have the fight.

And beyond.

"You too are strong. So much stronger than you thought you were. You will do what's right for Adelaide. I know that. And she does too." That was the last line of the email Courtney's mother, Lori, had written me, just days before she died. The same one in which she told me to have the fight.

She had been right.

About all of it.

And I was so fucking strong, but this next step was going to take a level of strength I didn't want to possess. My goal had always been to provide Adelaide with the best quality of life available to her. And conveniently, what had brought her peace and comfort had brought me the same. But like my great-grandmother Adelaide and her children before me, our paths were diverging. I didn't want to live a life without her, but there was no other way to give her the peace she deserved.

A week had passed since Alison's failed attempt at an end-of-life care conversation with me. Adelaide was screaming again, and we had already reached the maximum dosage of her over-the-counter pain medications.

"She needs stronger meds, Kelly. She needs hospice." Alison's tone was no longer pleading. It was intense, insistent.

After his own attempts at consoling Adelaide that morning, Miguel had retreated downstairs to hit golf balls into a DIY net. I was jealous of his ability to distract himself from our helpless situation, but also knew he was purposefully staying within ear shot should he be needed. At the sight of my tear-streaked face, Miguel stopped swinging his club.

"I think it's time for hospice," I told him.

In the late-night dark of our bedroom, we had discussed this transition several times. But in that safe space, it had been confined to the theoretical. Awash in daylight at the foot of our stairs, it was a reality. Miguel wasn't blind to this most recent decline; he also held her while she screamed, and I had watched him cry over her while she slept. But he was waiting for me to make the call.

Miguel said nothing. There was nothing left to say. Instead, he hugged me tightly as we cried onto each other's shoulder. It no longer mattered if I thought I was strong enough. Adelaide needed me to be. And both she and Lori believed I could be.

At our first hospice visit, the nurse explained that should Adelaide make a recovery, she could come off hospice. It was a sweet thought, but we both knew that was not going to happen. Their first task was to get Adelaide's pain under control—which would come at the cost of her remaining cognitive awareness.

Now we had to tell Jackson what was happening.

Tina, our hospice social worker, helped us make a plan. We decided to tell him the day before he was to start second grade in the hope that the new school year would provide a distraction. Then we called a family meeting, with all of us climbing onto Adelaide's twin bed.

"Adelaide's brain is really sick, monkey, and the doctors don't know how to fix it," I started.

"I know that already," Jackson said, feigning disinterest by playing with the quilt on her bed.

"Right, but now we know that she's not going to grow up and be a big kid like you. We don't know how long we have left with her but . . ." My throat tightened, protesting the rest of the sentence. *Deep breath. Say the words.* ". . . your sister is dying."

Tina had explained that it was important to use the "D-word" to give him the best chance at understanding. Jackson sat uncomfortably stoic on the bed. It was hard to tell what his seven-year-old psyche was comprehending. A steady stream of tears rolled down my cheeks, and I handed Miguel the book we had chosen to read to Jackson to help him process this news. Through tears of his own, Miguel read *The Memory Box* by Joanna Rowland, a book about a child who collects items that remind them of their lost loved one. Then I presented Jackson with craft supplies so that we could make a memory box together.

Shortly after our talk, Jackson started meeting with a child life specialist through the hospice team. She was someone he could talk to and play with, in the comfort of our home, and who could help him make sense of the inevitable. She integrated Adelaide into activities when it made sense but gave Jackson the individual emotional support he needed as well.

Despite our family entering hospice, life didn't stop for us. There were still back-to-school nights, little league baseball games, and Miguel's thousandth performance as Alexander Hamilton, which we celebrated with cake and bubbly. Meanwhile, our home was a revolving door of nurses, medication deliveries, and therapy specialists.

Because our apartment call box rang to my cell phone, Tabasco ran to the door every time my phone rang, assuming someone was there to see him. He was visibly disappointed when it was an actual phone call. Pavlov fail.

To get me out of the house for at least one hour each day, Jenny insisted on taking me to a workout class. I hate workout classes. But I had to admit it felt good to move my body. Jenny was driving me home after class and had just pulled onto our street when I got a call from Nurse Alison.

"Kelly, her oxygen rates are falling and none of the usual tricks are working. What do you want me to do?"

I read between her words. The DNR had been signed. She was asking if I wanted her to save my daughter's life.

"You tried her inhaler and upped her oxygen?"

I knew she had. I was stalling. *This isn't supposed to be happening yet.*

"Yes. I need you to tell me if you want me to use the ventilator."

When we entered hospice, I had decided to no longer use the awful machine because Adelaide hated it so much. It forced air into her lungs through a tube connected to a small mask that covered her nose.

Jenny pulled up in front of our apartment building.

"I'll be there in one minute, just hang on."

Jenny mouthed the words "call me" as I got out of the car, flying up the front stairs and into the building.

Adelaide was propped up in her bed, eyes closed, breathing shallowly, her color deceptively healthy. Despite her falling vitals, she looked peaceful. Alison was crouched beside her caressing her hair. Frank Sinatra played low in the background. I sat down next to Adelaide on the bed and held her hand.

"What do you want to do? You said before no ventilator, but I will do whatever you want me to." Alison was calm. *How is she so calm?*

I looked at the ladybug clock on the wall. It was 1:30 PM on a Wednesday, which meant Miguel had just stepped on stage to perform the matinee. There was no way he would make it home in time to say goodbye to her. But that wasn't the real reason.

I'm not ready, baby girl. Not yet, please not yet. I need more time.

"Let's do the ventilator."

Deftly, we moved together to get the mask secured around Adelaide's head. Within moments of the machine turning on, her vitals had stabilized. We had bought her time. But how much?

Call me, I texted Miguel.

As the adrenaline dissipated, my guilt grew. Guilt for going to a workout class, guilt for momentarily pretending my life was any kind of normal, but mostly guilt for not being strong enough to let Adelaide go. While Alison called the hospice team with the update, I called my mom.

"She was dying. We saved her, but I don't know if I should have."

"I'll be there as soon as I can."

Over the next twenty-four hours, losing Adelaide solidified from an abstract "someday" to a finite "any day." Mom arrived the next afternoon and took over basic household management, from meals to dishes to laundry, and I vowed never to leave Adelaide's side again.

CHAPTER EIGHTEEN
The Griever

While Adelaide was under hospice care, her bedroom had become our home's main living space. Using my laptop as a screen, Jackson lay with Adelaide watching movies. On Sundays, Miguel sat on the floor beside her bed watching football. I only left her side to shower and eat, choosing to sleep in her bed with her at night. I'm not sure she loved that part, but I didn't give her much of a choice.

Thanks to Mom, our nurses, and the hospice team, for two weeks I got to focus exclusively on being Adelaide's mother. We read *Guess How Much I Love You, Beauty and the Beast,* and all the Ladybug Girl books. I braided her hair and painted her nails. I tried to commit the shape and feel of her hands to memory. With Mom's help, I took copies of her fingerprint so that later I could have jewelry made with the print on them. I was no longer her nurse, or pharmacist, or physical therapist. I didn't worry about meals or if the dishes were clean. My only job was to love my child as much as possible, and *that* was the most precious gift I could have received.

Without a strict schedule to follow, time no longer adhered to the laws of physics: speeding up then slowing down, each day blending into the next. I felt untethered and adrift. But if Adelaide was the North Star by which our family's course was set, Jackson had become our lighthouse. I would be staring at Adelaide, wondering if her breathing was raspier today than yesterday or if her color was more sallow, and then out of nowhere Jackson would let out a rapturous, joy-filled giggle in the other room. Even amidst the most suffocating dark, he was bringing light into our home, never allowing us to drift too far from the shore. He guided our ship on this journey one fart joke and infectious laugh at a time.

Adelaide's fourth birthday was only three weeks away, but it seemed unlikely she would be with us to celebrate. It was also clear that the Make-A-Wish trip we had planned months earlier—Epilepsy Awareness Day at Disneyland in November—was not going to be happening. In its place, Adelaide's wish coordinator, with help from my cousins, pulled together a ladybug birthday party in under forty-eight hours, complete with a visit from Princess Belle. Just because we couldn't take Adelaide to Disney didn't mean we couldn't bring Disney to Adelaide.

"Hello Adelaide, my name is Princess Belle, and I hear we are celebrating your birthday today!"

Adelaide peeked in the direction of this new singsongy voice.

"I've brought a special story I would like to read you. Would you like that?"

Adelaide opened her eyes wider than I had seen in months. *Beauty and the Beast* was in our regular book rotation, and she had watched the movie countless times. I'd doubted Adelaide would have any real recognition of this person sitting beside her, yet here she was, in pure wonderment, even vocalizing in the princess's direction.

"Adelaidey! Are you so excited to be meeting Princess Belle?" I laughed in awe that my incredible daughter could still surprise me.

For the next several minutes, Adelaide gazed at Belle as the princess read her the story of how she went from being the daughter of an inventor to a princess in an enchanted castle. By the time the story was over and we sang "Happy Birthday," Adelaide had returned to her internal world, exhausted by her efforts. But for a moment, one unbelievably magical moment, she had been present and with us again.

Two excruciating weeks later, and just five days before her fourth birthday, Adelaide passed away at home in my arms, surrounded by her daddy, grandma, and so much love. It was as peaceful a moment as I could have imagined—had this ever been a scenario I forced myself to imagine. My only regret is that I didn't take a picture of her after she died. I know that sounds morbid, and that's why I didn't do it when I felt the initial urge, but the strain or pain that had lived in her face was gone. It had become such a part of her appearance that I hadn't recognized it for what it was until it was no longer there.

If only it hadn't taken death for her to experience peace.

THERE HAD BEEN more significant detours in my life than I ever could have anticipated. But each blockade, each crater, had come with a new, more pressing purpose—or at least a distraction. Until this one.

When Adelaide died, the road forward ceased to exist. I found myself at a precipice. No, "a precipice" gives the impression that I could go back, or maybe find a way around. This was like being stranded on an island surrounded by a vast emptiness.

It wasn't just my grief that bound me to my island. I had no idea who I was supposed to be or what I was supposed to do without Adelaide. There was no new purpose to ferry me through the transition. No path to forge, no current to lead me. Any bridge, had I the energy to build one, would have led to nowhere.

One day I had been coordinating care, responding to alarms, and monitoring medications. The next I awoke achingly aware that the bedroom next to mine was empty and there was nothing I *had* to do. It was like I'd been fired from a job I loved, forced into an early retirement at thirty-seven years old.

Even though I had spent the last few weeks watching her slip away. Even though I knew this morning was inevitable. Even though I had experienced, survived, and thrived through several drastic life changes before. Nothing could prepare me for this.

She was here, and then she wasn't.

I had held her, and now I couldn't.

I'd known what I had to do, and now I didn't.

My senses were dulled by grief, as if I was neither fully asleep nor awake. Like I was dreaming, my focus narrowed to whatever I could see directly in front of me. My peripheral vision blurred. I read the condolence cards piling up on the counter and looked at the various gifts we'd been sent—drawings, photo collages, a wind chime—before boxing them up and putting them away to be sorted through on a future day by a future me. In some ways, planning Adelaide's service was a gift, in that it gave me something to do. We chose the songs to be sung by Miguel's *Hamilton* castmates. With the help of Broadway In Chicago, the local producing partner for *Hamilton*, we secured a venue and put out a press release.

A fucking press release.

The same newspapers, networks, and websites that had followed Miguel for the last three years, the publications whose racks I had passed when picking up Adelaide's medications, the stations we had begged to let us talk about epilepsy—they would all now run a piece about our daughter's passing.

I imagined people reading it on their phones, or hearing about it as they drank their morning coffee. They would feel bad for us, and then they would swipe up to the next story in their feed. I wanted to swipe up too, but my phone was broken.

Call it coincidence, or luck, or a shitstorm of epic proportions, but Adelaide and *Hamilton*'s intertwinement wasn't over. Just a few days after Adelaide died, while we were out picking up supplies for her memorial service, Miguel answered a call from *Hamilton*'s producer and director. They asked if he would like to transfer to the New York *Hamilton* company after the Chicago company closed in January.

I resisted the urge to find meaning in any of these closely tied events. What did it matter?

"Congratulations, babe," I told him.

"I'd give it all up if we could have her back," Miguel said.

"I know."

Any other time, this news would have been celebrated. A job! On Broadway! We would have felt relief to know what our next steps would be. But now, after building a community that loved and supported us, that knew and loved our daughter, that helped us create four years of memories in Chicago as a family of four, we would be leaving—as a family of three.

My grief was quickly becoming the nastiest tangle of string lights you've ever seen. Tiny spikes pushing through wires, looped over other wires, stuck on more lights. Every string that was pulled just drew the knots tighter. Understanding grief, processing it, and untangling the wires would be painstaking work. I was yearning for a task, a project, a purpose—but tackling this seemingly endless ball of lightless bulbs wasn't it.

I tried to resist my grief by barreling forward with life and any plans I had made prior to Adelaide's death. I accepted an award for my blog in Las Vegas. Alongside Miguel and Jackson, I attended and spoke at Epilepsy Awareness Day at Disneyland, the very event that was supposed to be Adelaide's Make-A-Wish trip. Jackson donned ladybug wings as our family waved from the back of a convertible in the Chicago Thanksgiving Parade.

But when it came time to make plans for our move back east, I delayed Jackson's and my departure. I reasoned that Jackson should be allowed to finish second grade in Chicago . . . and then we should remain there through the summer because you don't survive a Chicago winter not to enjoy the summer. Miguel would go back to New Jersey in February to start work, then travel back and forth to visit us on his days off.

First, though, he had to finish out the rest of the Chicago run. Two weeks after Adelaide's death, Miguel returned to work. I attended his first performance back in case he couldn't make it through the show and needed to leave. However, Miguel made it through just fine. In fact, Miguel always seemed to be fine. He was grieving, of course, but he appeared so much less affected than I was. Part of me was grateful, because his togetherness created space for me to fall apart. But also I didn't get it. How was he so okay? An all-too-familiar resentment grew inside me. Like with Elvis, and while caring for Adelaide, here we were again: why was the distribution of our shared trauma so uneven?

Had you asked me before Adelaide died who I thought would provide me the most comfort in my grief I would have answered without hesitation: Miguel. We had navigated so much stress and anguish together already. Up to that point, our emotional responses had usually been in sync. I hadn't considered how differently we might respond to Adelaide's death and how that would affect our ability to rely on each other in grief.

I would be slumped on the bathroom floor, heaving with sobs. I knew that Miguel knew where I was and what I was doing there, but he rarely came to check on me. If it was an especially long grief exorcism, he might knock on the door, but he rarely came inside, sat with me, or held me. Meanwhile, as time went on, I rarely witnessed Miguel fall apart. I felt so alone in my grief—broken, and like I didn't even fit in my own home.

In couple's counseling, I learned that just because I wasn't seeing Miguel express his grief didn't mean he wasn't grieving. He just preferred to let it out when he was alone. Because of that, he assumed that I also wanted to be alone when my grief werewolf took over.

"Sometimes I just really need a hug," I told him.

With the counselor's help, we agreed that I would tell him what I needed from him in terms of comfort, and he would tell me when he had been grieving after the fact. It wasn't a perfect system and felt awkward at the start, but over time it became more natural.

Even still, I felt like I needed so much more comfort, grace, patience, and time. So often I wanted to be held and seen, loved and cared for. I had been looking to Miguel for all of this, but that wasn't fair: he had lost his daughter too. He wasn't in need the same way that I was, but he also couldn't carry me alone.

Once Miguel was back at work, his visible displays of grief became even rarer. He has admitted to me that he felt guilty because he recognized that he had somewhere to go, somewhere he was needed. He got to escape the shadow that hung over our home and pretend to be someone else for hours—just as he had on Adelaide's bad days during her life.

Even though in the show he was playing a character whose son dies, "that's not my kid that dies on stage every night," he'd say. It was a distraction and a job, and a role he had performed over a thousand times. I never questioned his desire to return to the show. It made sense to me: onstage he had purpose, was valued, and special. All things I felt like I lost with Adelaide. If I'd been able to return to a job where I was valued, maybe my grief would have been easier to manage too. Or, who knows, maybe the additional stress and necessary emotional suppression would have made it all worse. The answer is irrelevant. There was no use in comparing our grieving styles. What mattered was doing our best to support each other to the best of our abilities.

While Miguel was not a great comforter, I never felt judged by him for how much more visible my grief was than his. He never pushed me to feel less or to move through it more quickly. He never insinuated that my grief was too much or inconvenient or uncomfortable. He let me feel what I was feeling without judgement, which was an invaluable kind of support on its own.

So Miguel was back at work, Jackson was back in school, and I was back in bed. But only after my morning workout class, which Jenny insisted on picking me up for daily. Much like the first time she had invited me to her home, when it came to these classes she was not taking no for an answer.

"Mornin'!" Jenny greeted me as I opened her car door.

I responded with a disgusted face and a curled lip. Just because I was going with her to class didn't mean I had to like it. Though I did appreciate knowing that if I did nothing else that day, at least I had done something.

"Your hand is shaking. Did you take your meds this morning?" Jenny asked.

At the urging of Mom and Jenny, I had started seeing a psychiatrist, who had prescribed antidepressants. Jenny chauffeured me to those appointments as well, to be sure I didn't miss them—accidentally or otherwise.

"Yes, I took my meds. I don't think I ate anything, though."

"There's a protein bar in my bag. Now let's get pumped!" And with that, she pulled a U-ey into traffic while blasting Eminem . . . at 9 AM.

God, I hated those classes, but I was endlessly grateful for the company and support Jenny provided me. What Miguel struggled to offer me in grief, Jenny filled in, teaching me a lesson that probably saved our marriage: it's okay if your romantic partner doesn't meet all of your emotional needs. Sometimes, you have to outsource. As I wrote in my first book, *Normal Broken*, "If your person-in-chief didn't know how to fix a broken pipe, you wouldn't get mad at them—you would call a plumber."

Jenny was my plumber, who laid with me in bed while I cried, and then would crack a joke to get me out of bed again. She knew which friends brought me comfort and which ones, though well-meaning, did anything but, and helped keep them at bay—all while she was grieving Adelaide too. Jenny had been the first person to call me the morning after her death, the first person I had to tell.

But Jenny had already known. "She's gone, isn't she?" Jenny said softly. "I couldn't feel her energy in the world anymore."

THREE MONTHS AFTER Adelaide died, and nearly three and a half years after we moved halfway across the country for Miguel to lead the cast, *Hamilton* closed in Chicago. I remember the bittersweet energy of that final weekend and being surrounded by friends and family, but the rest is like an out-of-focus photograph. Life was moving too fast for my sluggish lens to keep up.

And then it was time for Miguel to pack his bags and head back to New Jersey. We had bought a new house there that Mig would move into and slowly get ready for Jackson's and my arrival at the end of the summer. I was simultaneously offended that life was still happening and relieved by its distractions.

Then, less than a month later, on Thursday, March 12, 2020, I was at a CURE Epilepsy board meeting in Chicago when Miguel texted me from New York that Broadway was being shut down due to COVID-19. He was only ten performances into his New York contract. The next morning, he boarded a plane using a scarf for a mask and flew back to Chicago to wait out what we all thought would be a two-week hiatus.

The pandemic would force many a personal reckoning as it changed the entire world, and our shrunken household would be no exception. Specifically, we would return to New Jersey earlier than planned, since without Miguel's income we could no longer afford to pay two mortgages. It was yet another goodbye exacted before I was ready. And on July 7, 2020, we left Chicago, our community, and our friends to move back to New Jersey, into a home Adelaide would never know.

CHAPTER NINETEEN
The Writer

As the one-year anniversary of Adelaide's death approached, I felt a sort of mania take hold of me. I had felt like a purposeless shell for too long, cracked in a hundred places and in constant risk of shattering. I wanted to get to a point in time where I felt like me again.

That was the problem, though: I would never again be the "me" I was when Adelaide was alive. Just like I would never be the person I was when I was working full-time in New York City, or when I was flying around the country visiting Miguel while he was on tour, or when I was overachieving my way through college. Those versions were all still tucked away inside me, and they had shaped me, but I would never inhabit them again.

Over the last year, I had drunk my way through my birthday and had a panic attack on the highway, at the grocery store, and at a child's birthday party. I sent Miguel out alone to meet our new neighbors and tell them our story, protecting me from certain public self-immolation. I took a nap every day, and sometimes two, because the days were too long to survive without breaks. Tabasco's fur absorbed more tears than the dozens of tissue boxes I went through. I diligently took my antidepressant medication so, at the very least, I could still show up for Jackson. And then when I remembered, I tried to acknowledge my inchstones. I found that the practice of "inchstones not milestones" that had helped me refocus energy during Adelaide's life applied to life without her as well. They were the small steps I took beyond simply surviving toward something that resembled living, even if those steps were as small as brushing my teeth.

I knew I should want to heal because that was what all the grief books Mom sent me assumed I wanted. But I equated healing with moving on and letting go, neither of which interested me or seemed remotely feasible. Still, I was tired of feeling stuck, depressed, and out of control. I wanted to hit fast-forward to a time in life where I was right side up, or at least knew which direction up was. Without a universal life remote, I made the next best decision: buying another dog.

Oh, was that not where you thought this was going? Well, grief is rarely rational, and this wasn't exactly the first time I'd brought home a puppy in the midst of an identity crisis. Tabasco was still in good health, but as he neared twelve, his inevitable mortality was haunting me. And besides, with Tabasco's sworn fealty to me, Jackson had been begging for a dog of his own for years now. Over the summer and fall, I applied to dozens of rescue agencies. Unfortunately, it was the height of the pandemic, and so everyone else was doing the same. But as Adelaide's deathiversary grew closer, I willingly sacrificed logic and reason for a fluffy dose of serotonin. I left the rescue sites and started looking at breeders, but those waits were a year or longer. And then I found a listing for bernedoodle puppies a couple hours away. I made a call, placed a hold on one of the puppies, and two days later, Jackson, Mom, and I were on the road.

I had warned Jackson that if it felt like they were abusing the puppies in any way or if it was some kind of puppy mill, we would go home with an empty crate. Instead, we pulled up to a modest farmhouse, and a sweet family came outside to greet us before leading us to a fenced area on the side of the yard where the black, brown, and white pups were being kept during the day. Their mother, a Bernese, was dozing in the sun in the grass nearby. As we approached, the puppies excitedly climbed on top of each other like adorable, fuzzy zombies, trying to reach us. The couple's school-aged daughter helped Jackson wrangle one of the puffballs, a girl, away from her scrappy siblings.

In keeping with our hot sauce theme, we had told Jackson he could name his dog whatever he wanted, as long as it was Sriracha or Cholula. I had been campaigning for Cholula, but Sriracha won out.

To be clear, Racha—as she is now called—was not my best decision. Jackson would disagree and still looks back on that day as one of the best of his life. My shoes, couch cushions, underwear, dozens of remote controls, and countless socks beg to differ. Everyone told me it was a phase, that I should "give her chew toys, and she'll grow out of it!" Four years later, we are still taking our couch cushions to be mended and finding sock remnants in her poop.

While I don't recommend manically adding animals to your family, it was a step. Even if not forward, it at least counted as movement. Movement that gave me the courage to start purging, and this time, not the contents of my stomach. I started with the trunk of children's toys, which had initially traveled with us from New Jersey to Chicago. Was it wishful thinking? Naivety? Denial? I had been so sure we would be able to use its contents eventually. Closer to the truth was that I couldn't imagine a life where they were never needed.

Years in Chicago went by, and the trunk was moved to a storage unit where it would collect expensive dust—still holding the remnants of dreams that I knew would never come to pass but that I still couldn't release. The trunk would come to gather even more expensive dust as it was transported cross-country again to our home in New Jersey. Rarely touched and never opened.

In the days before that first deathiversary, I found myself needing to feel the sharp edges of my grief. Finally, I brought myself to open the trunk. I pushed the silver lock, releasing the heavy-hinged lid, and pulled it open. Inside lay a plastic cornucopia of brightly colored toys. A mix of what had once been Jackson's favorite playthings and a few of my own that Mom had passed on to me several years before Adelaide was born. Miniature pots and pans, tiny animal figurines, building blocks, and a large, chocolate-brown Pound Puppy complete with doghouse, heart-shaped red bowl, and bone. Her name, "Jessica"—an '80s classic—was spelled out in individual letter stickers on the front of the red and blue plastic house.

A lifetime ago, a different Kelly had saved all these toys for Adelaide. I had accepted that Adelaide's inability to play with these toys was irrelevant to her happiness, but my emotions were still caught in a culturally programmed loop of what childhood was supposed to look like, and these toys were part of it. I had struggled to let them go.

A few days later, sitting at my desk overlooking our front yard, I watched a little girl enjoy her tree swing across the street. Her blonde hair whipped in the wind as she spun in circles. She was five, the same age Adelaide would have been.

Without letting myself think too much about it, I returned to the trunk and lifted the lid.

"Ruby!" I yelled from our doorstep to the girl on the swing. Crossing the street, I kept my hands behind my back. "I have a present for you." Ruby leapt from her swing as I revealed the Pound Puppy doghouse along with Jessica, her food bowl, and bone.

Ruby's face lit up. Smiling ecstatically, she ran back to her house with her treasure before turning around briefly. "Thank you!" she yelled. I like to imagine a *Toy Story*-esque scene playing out with Jessica being introduced to the rest of the toys in Ruby's room.

Giving away the toys, and in turn releasing the dreams I'd held onto for Adelaide, didn't lessen my grief. I did, however, find it empowering. It was an action I could take, something to do that gave me strength.

And it was significantly less expensive and more effective than impulsively adding animals to our family.

As goal-oriented as I am, I started to understand that my grief would always be a part of me. There would be no finish line, no pizza party. I would always be grieving, never grieved. Instead of feeling like I'd been given a Sisyphean curse, I found comfort in this knowledge. It was like the analogy of grief as a rock in your pocket: at first it weighs you down so intensely it feels like you're drowning. But in time, you become stronger, and the rock's weight grows less noticeable. Nowadays, I like to put my hand in my pocket and hold the rock. Rubbing its now-smooth sides for comfort, it is my proof that Adelaide was here.

But only one year in, the weight was still a strain. It wasn't as crushing as it had been in those earliest weeks and months, but it still affected my every action, thought, and breath. The difference was that I no longer clung to the rock as if it was the only thing keeping me afloat in a vast nothingness. A life with the rock, not for the rock, was starting to take shape.

It was still blurry, but the outlines were there.

At only thirty-eight, my working life was not over. But I was struggling to figure out what I wanted to do in this fourth iteration of my career. After praying that I wouldn't get cast from the couple of self-tape auditions I submitted through my old commercial agent, I realized that wasn't where my interests lay. My worldview had been too far altered to work in events or restaurants again—there was no number of acting classes that could help me pretend to care about the corporate planner who was angry that the buffet wasn't full enough. Nor did I have the energy to mediate a dispute between a maid of honor and the mother of the bride over a bridal shower brunch menu. We were also still in a global pandemic, and even if I had been able to suck it up for a paycheck, neither restaurants nor events were exactly booming industries.

I felt exceedingly fortunate (dare I say lucky?) that we weren't in dire need of my income. I had time to figure this out. Eventually, Broadway would reopen, and while we were currently living off savings, we wouldn't be forever. I wanted to make a living again both to take the pressure off Miguel and because making money feels good. I was ready to feel some good.

But what was I even capable of with such a dense grief rock weighing me down?

A scholarly friend would later teach me that, in medieval times, "rock" was a much more specific concept than it is today. Rocks were immovable and composed of many other geological components. Stones, on the other hand, were smaller and made up of a single component with specific uses.

Could I break my grief rock apart into stones—into the inchstones I'd personally gathered while caring for Adelaide? There were my advocacy and board positions, the podcast I hosted for CURE Epilepsy, my blog and the social media presence I had carved out amongst the epilepsy, disability, and grief communities. When viewed as a rock, my grief was fixed and awkward, but if it were broken apart, I could redistribute the weight—perhaps even use it positively.

There was something there; I just wasn't sure what exactly. What if I could get up on stage and tell our story? What if I could I write a book? With nothing but time, I hired a writing coach and worked with her weekly. I started to read with a different focus: not just for enjoyment, but to learn and enhance my own writing. This wasn't a career yet, but it was something—a goal, maybe even a dream.

Since moving to New Jersey, I had struggled to find a therapist who I connected with and would ask me the questions that challenged my fears and interpretations of them. But when I sat down at my computer to write, I saw my life from an aerial view. I saw the obstacles and the opened doors, the craters and the ways I'd moved around them. I could also see that my desolate grief island was actually a peninsula.

There was a path forward—but it wasn't pleasant. I was going to have to hike carefully and work through a lot of branches and brambles, so as not to slip into the depths of my grief. I started writing every day for hours, emerging only for coffee, Miguel's breakfast tacos, and to pee. I wrote about Adelaide's birth and early life. I wrote about every ambulance ride, diagnosis, and doctor. I wrote about the helplessness of uncontrolled epilepsy and the blind panic followed by unearthly calm that I experienced watching my daughter be resuscitated time and time again.

I wrote about Adelaide's life, and how she showed me that empathy was a superpower, that communication went far beyond verbal ability, and that disability wasn't a bad word. And then I wrote about her death with as much detail as I had her birth. When I was done, I had composed a 63,000–word manuscript of my daughter's life through my eyes.

The night before his inauguration, President Joe Biden gave a speech at a COVID-19 memorial ceremony. Regardless of your political leanings, you've got to recognize that this man knows grief; he lost his wife and infant daughter in a car crash and then an adult son to brain cancer. In his speech, he said, "To heal, we must remember."

No words have rung truer for me in my grief journey. As painful as it was to relive Adelaide's life, it was what I needed to do to begin healing. Instead of moving on and forgetting, I needed to create and remember. When I was writing about Adelaide, I got to live in a world where she was alive. I got to bring her with me into the present. In doing so, I created the ultimate weapon against my greatest adversary: the memory thief known as time. I knew my memories of her would fade—not all of them, and not in totality, but inevitably, they would. However, once they were recorded, I could always revisit them.

Some of those stories made their way into this book, others into my previous book, *Normal Broken*. Writing had created my path toward healing. It would be my defense against time.

CHAPTER TWENTY
The Hopeful

Ever since Elvis, I had looked at pregnant women I passed on the street with a mix of jealousy and disdain. How nice for them to be pregnant, but did they know how many things could go wrong? How healthy babies were not a guarantee? How sometimes you rolled sevens and other times you rolled snake eyes?

For years, during our late-night, postcoital talks, Mig and I had discussed adding to our family. But not having a diagnosis for Adelaide seriously complicated matters. There was no way to know if our next baby would survive childhood. And given our track record, I did not feel like the odds were in our favor. I also had zero interest in being pregnant again. Physically, emotionally, hormonally, traumatically . . . just no. Still, having the decision effectively taken from me—because I wasn't willing to take a chance on another baby's health—was yet another complicated loss.

While Adelaide was still alive, Miguel and I had explored adoption. And by explore, I mean we did a few Google searches and talked to some friends. We quickly learned how challenging it can be to adopt an American baby and watched multiple friends experience heartbreak in the process. From a birth mother changing her mind at the last minute to waiting years for a birth mother to choose you out of a pile of other applicants—this was a level of stress I wasn't ready to subject myself to. We briefly considered fostering to adopt, but the goal of foster care is reunification with the birth family, not adoption. If protecting our family from additional heartbreak was a priority, then foster care was not for us.

By the time we moved our quarantining headquarters from our couch in Chicago to our couch in New Jersey, I was trying to convince myself that our physical family of three could be enough. Pandemic aside, life was relatively low-stress for a change, and maybe that was nice. But then as the world began to wake from COVID dormancy, my earlier interest in adoption was reborn as well.

All three of us knew something was missing, and it wasn't just Adelaide. She left a void that could not be filled or erased—a space that will only ever be hers and hers alone. This was something else. It was a yearning for more love and to give more love, and in the rare moments I gave into the feeling and let my mind wander down its winding path of possibilities, I came away clutching fistfuls of hope.

Hope. A feeling as foreign to me as a life without loss. Hope wasn't rational, and in order to get this far in my healing journey, I had needed to dig my nails into what was real. But hope felt good, and I was surprised at how starved I was for it.

In hindsight, I probably should have seen this coming when I drove to another state to impulsively buy a dog and then was shocked when she didn't make everything better. To be clear, I love my dogs immensely, but they are not the same as children.

"What if we looked into adopting internationally?" I asked Miguel one morning. This conversation needed to happen in daylight. I needed to see his face, to suss out his true feelings on the subject.

If I caught him by surprise, he wasn't showing it. His face remained steady, open.

"That could be cool. Maybe from a Spanish-speaking country?"

"Yeah." I took a few breaths as a new future unfolded before us. "I need a hug."

Miguel took me in his arms and held me until I was sated.

Two days, many hours of research, and a couple of phone calls later, we signed with an agency to adopt a child from Colombia. If I was concerned by our repeated impulsivity, I was also soothed by the number of classes, level of effort, and amount of time it would take before any adoption would be finalized.

And so began a new kind of pregnancy. One that involved social workers, home inspections, early childhood trauma training, and educating ourselves on Colombian culture. The adoption agency's checklist added purpose to my days. I once again had direction, a goal, and something to look forward to.

I STOOD IN front of the full-length mirror in the corner of our bedroom, trying to take a picture of my reflection, but the light wasn't great and I couldn't figure out a way to stand that was flattering while also blocking the clutter of clothing and hangars littering my bed like a mulled-over clearance bin. It didn't help that nothing fit. It had been well over a year since I had been expected to dress up for anything. I could blame grief, the pandemic, aging hormones, or my psych meds—regardless, I had gained twenty pounds and no amount of shapewear was going to enable the necessary zippering.

I knew my body felt different, that my face looked fuller in photographs, but my former obsession with my weight barely registered anymore. All my energy was now spent on Jackson, the adoption, and trying not to be too awkward when I met new people. Which, now that COVID restrictions were lifting, was becoming more and more common.

With help from a stylish friend via texted photos, I decided on a simple, and most importantly, zipperless black slip dress. I was grateful that tonight, as Broadway reopened after eighteen months of empty theaters and dark stages, no one would be paying much attention to me.

After a quick bite at one of the few theater district restaurants not shuttered as a result of the pandemic, Miguel, Jackson, and I walked hand in hand down 46th Street to the theater as the sun set behind us. Eventually we made it past the crowds, news cameras, and vaccine and mask checks to our seats. The crowd hummed with an energy akin to an opening night and with all the corresponding glitz and glamour. The air was full of hope—the sense that maybe, just maybe, life was finally progressing toward a new, less socially restrictive normal.

Jackson and I hollered and applauded at Miguel's stage entrance. No one would be shaming me for disturbing their experience during this performance. Sitting amongst an audience celebrating collective survival and resilience, I couldn't help but acknowledge all the pain, processing, and healing that had brought us to this moment, wearing this zipless dress, sitting next to my beautiful son, while watching my husband create magic on stage.

"I noticed you cheering for the guy playing Hamilton; do you know him?" asked the young woman sitting next to me at intermission.

"He's my husband," I answered while opening a bag of Twizzlers for Jackson. A sugar boost was the only way to be sure he stayed awake during the second act. I looked up at her and gave her my well-rehearsed, if dusty, proud-wife smile.

"Oh! He's amazing," she said, her eyes opening wide.

"Thank you. It feels good to see him onstage again."

"I'm going to school for musical theater; a show like this is my dream. You're so lucky."

Lucky?

I looked away, nursing the rage and resentment pulsing through my veins. Were we lucky when our daughter died? When we had to move away from the community that knew our daughter best? When we were unemployed and living off savings for the last eighteen months?

"I'm not sure how much luck has to do with it," I said. I forced another smile and turned toward Jackson, effectively ending the conversation.

I steadied myself with a few deep breaths. Jackson instinctively grabbed my hand, attuned to my mood change, and scanned my face for the latest trigger. I squeezed his hand to reassure him that I was okay.

"I love you," I told him.

"I love you more," he replied.

"That's just not possible," I countered.

I continued to ground myself against the irrational: I felt the carpet beneath my stiletto heels and the cushioned auditorium seating supporting my body, saw the magnificent chandelier floating above my head. This theater, the Richard Rodgers, held so many of our family's memories. Like ghostly vignettes, the scenes played out before me: Jackson, age two, singing "The ABCs" center stage with his dad under a spotlight during Miguel's run in *If/Then*. Miguel chasing Jackson up the mezzanine stairs after a front-row pizza picnic while I looked on, cradling Elvis in my barely bulging tummy.

There were the seats I squeezed into while eight months pregnant with Adelaide when Miguel and I watched *Hamilton* for the first time. (How unaware we had been of the ways this show and the child I was carrying would change our lives!) I saw Lin-Manuel Miranda, in front of the mezzanine seats, singing "Adelaide" from *Guys and Dolls* to our Adelaide when she was eight months old during a *Hamilton* rehearsal. And over there was where Mom and I sat at Miguel's first performance when she'd asked me with a wink if he got to bring the costumes home.

These memories were undeniably sweet. But were they sweet enough to balance out the sour? After all, no one's life is good all the time. If the sweet in our life was the result of a lucky roll of the dice, how much of it had we already gambled away? And what was the currency we had been gambling with? Because every time we seemed to win, the house kept asking us to pay up even more.

Sitting in that theater watching my husband perform for a sold-out audience with my son by my side, I knew we were okay. We were going to be okay. That we were surviving was a testament to our collective choice to heal. Healing took effort. But luck did not—and that was what had hurt me so much about the young woman's comment. She only saw in our family the effortless and sweet; she was missing the sweat and the sour. She was missing all it had taken to get to this place. If what she saw was luck, she was missing all that we paid for it. She was missing Adelaide.

Wait, stop; that's not right. That makes it seem like Adelaide's memory is painful, and that's not true. Well, not entirely true. My grief for the life I had imagined for her, for us, for her suffering, and eventually for her physical body—that was painful. But it was only made painful because of the love and joy she brought into our lives. I had needed my pain and despair to be witnessed because it was all-consuming and because it was the only way I could make sure she was remembered at that time. But pain was not the conduit through which I wanted to honor my daughter. I wanted her legacy to be comforting, proactive, and hopeful.

There was that word again: hope.

I will never be the person who can always look on the bright side, who turns every lemon into lemonade—not because I don't want to be, but because sometimes there are just too many damn lemons to keep up. But what if I had the recipe wrong? What if the balance to the sour, to the despair, wasn't joy (be it forced or natural), but hope?

One of my favorite movies growing up was *The NeverEnding Story*. (Yes, I had a massive crush on Atreyu. Moving on.) In the movie, the Nothing threatens to wipe out the fictional world of Fantasia. When the aforementioned heartthrob Atreyu asks what the Nothing is, he is told, "It's the emptiness that's left. It's like a despair, destroying this world."

"But why?" Atreyu asks.

"Because people who have no hopes are easy to control; and whoever has the control . . . has the power."

In despair, I was powerless. Powerless over my present emotions, my future decisions, and the way my past (i.e., Adelaide) was remembered. When I dared to let myself hope and dream, instead of succumbing to nightmares, I felt myself strengthen. Hope is possibility and desire; it is love and acknowledgment. Giving myself permission to hope pushed away my despair like a flame does darkness. It also provided the light I needed to see and celebrate the joy that already existed in my life.

This didn't mean I was ready to open my own lemonade factory. The light also didn't make compost of the heaping piles of rotten lemons at my feet. But in that moment, celebrating the return of theater, watching my husband with my empathetic son my by side, I was choosing to bask in the warmth of that light. To appreciate the lemonade.

This life could be good. And so could Adelaide's memory.

CHAPTER TWENTY-ONE
The Luckiest (Reprise)

After growing accustomed to a slower pace of life during the pandemic, I now felt as if life was happening all at once. Two months after Broadway reopened, Jackson, Miguel, and I were on our way to the New York Stock Exchange to ring the closing bell alongside CURE Epilepsy employees and donors in a kickoff event for Epilepsy Awareness Month. The way Adelaide and *Hamilton* continued to overlap in our lives never ceased to amaze me. Here we were honoring Adelaide and all those impacted by epilepsy at the heart of the very financial system Alexander Hamilton created.

While waiting for the train, I asked Jackson to take a selfie with me. In addition to the pressure in the air from the threatening rain clouds behind us, I felt the framed photo of Adelaide in my purse weighing on my shoulder. Since Adelaide couldn't be with us, her photo would have to suffice.

We so often think of the moments when the course of our life is changed forever. But what about the moments before? Our memory swallows them up in the jarring impact that follows. But I still have that photo of Jackson and me, smiling on the train platform, excited for a break from the monotony of life in lockdown.

The train arrived, and Miguel and I settled into a three-seat bench with Jackson nestled between us. Only a few stops had passed by when Miguel stood up to answer a phone call. Jackson leaned against my shoulder, lulled by the swaying of the train, and I gazed out at the industrial swampland rolling past the window. Many parts of New Jersey are worthy of its "Garden State" moniker, but this stretch was not one of them. I waited for Miguel to wrap up the call and rejoin us, but when I was finally able to catch his gaze, I sensed a profound shift in his energy.

"Are you okay?" I mouthed to him.

He briefly shook his head in response. *Does that mean something is wrong? Or is he just shaking me off?* Patience is not a virtue to which I lay any sort of claim, and by the time Miguel sat back down with us, I was moments from anticipatory combustion.

"That was Martin." Miguel paused to look at Jackson, who was now asleep on my shoulder. He continued, but in a whisper, "Child Protective Services called him asking if he or any family members would be able to take Julie's kids."

"Take . . . as in adopt?" I asked.

"I don't know. I think so?" Miguel stared at the phone in his hands as if it might have the answers.

Julie was part of our family on Miguel's side. She had given birth to her first child just six months after I'd had Jackson—the difference being that I was thirty at the time and she was just sixteen. Over the next eight years, more children followed. However, the details of Julie's journey are not mine to tell. All that matters to *this* story is that a family was breaking apart and there were children in need of a new home, a ton of support, and a hell of a lot of love.

Between our geographical distance from Texas and our focus on Adelaide, we had not been kept up to date on Julie's life. Though I hadn't exactly been fighting for updates either. It was hard hearing that she had delivered *another* healthy baby when all I wanted was for my own to survive.

"Where are the children now?" I asked Miguel.

He shrugged. "I don't know."

"Where is Julie?"

"Houston, maybe?"

"When are they being removed?"

"I don't know." Miguel was getting more agitated with each question I asked, but I couldn't stop myself.

"What will this process look like?"

"Kelly, I don't know," Miguel said in a now-forced whisper, looking to Jackson to make sure he was actually asleep and not just playing possum like his sister used to do. "Martin said he would call back this evening with a caseworker who could explain more."

Over the next few days, we pieced together the situation through calls with family (including Julie), caseworkers, and a lawyer we hired to help advise us. It was decided that we would take custody of two-and-a-half-year-old Anessa and eventually start the legal process to adopt her. Then, Friday morning, just five days after we received the initial call from Martin, Miguel, Jackson, and I boarded a plane to Texas.

Thanks in part to the trauma training we had undertaken in preparation for our now-paused Colombian adoption, I was aware that there was a lot more to adoption than matching a child in need with a family in want. For a child to be available for adoption and a new family to be created, another family must break apart. And that was what we witnessed in an unadorned conference room, hauntingly similar to the one that had shattered our family with confirmation of Adelaide's neurodegeneration three years earlier. While tear-stained papers were signed, Julie's children played under the conference table, unaware of the custodial decisions being made inches above them.

The trauma of that excruciating hour still reverberates in my cells like an out-of-tune chord. I wanted to hide in a bathroom stall with my knees pulled up to my chest, to cry and scream against the suffocating pain in that room. But instead, I sat there silently, signing where I was told, and bore witness to another family's shattering.

Adoption can be beautiful. But like so much in the world, before it can be beautiful it is pain. Just as grief is born of love, adoption is born of loss.

The sun was trying to force its way through the clouds as I strapped Anessa into our rental car. Jackson was already buckled in, returned to us after a playdate with cousins meant to shield him as much as possible from the afternoon's pain. He was eager to give Anessa an enormous Minnie Mouse stuffed animal he had picked out from Target the night before and carried with him on the airplane that morning. For a moment, her eyes lit up as she received the gift with one hand while holding Jackson's hand in her other.

"Anessa, honey, are you hungry? Would you like to stop for ice cream?" I asked twisting around in the front passenger seat. The brief light in her eyes had dimmed again, and she didn't respond. I wasn't even entirely sure she had heard me.

"Is she having a seizure?" Miguel's eyes were darting from the rearview mirror to the road in front of him. Our own trauma on full display.

"Jackson, will you squeeze her hand?" I asked.

"She squeezed back," he said calmly, not taking his eyes off his new sister.

"Okay, so probably not a seizure, just, you know, life-altering trauma." I turned back around in my seat and took a few deep breaths.

Miguel took my hand in his and kissed it. "I love you," he told me.

"I love you too."

Anessa had just been separated from the only family she had ever known and passed off to strangers. At two and a half, it would be years before she understood what had just happened to her. For the rest of the day, she refused all food and drink and only responded to yes-or-no questions—and even then, only sparingly, with a nod or head shake. It wasn't until breakfast the next morning that she seemed to fully register our existence.

Remaining leery of Miguel and I, Anessa gravitated toward Jackson, who in turn reveled in the return of his big brother status.

"Want to get some breakfast?" Jackson asked his new little sister.

Anessa nodded in response before chasing Jackson down the hallway toward the hotel's breakfast room. When we met up with them in the buffet line, Anessa was enthusiastically pointing toward a bowl of fruit.

"Strawbabies! Strawbabies!" she exclaimed. It was the first word she had spoken since we'd met her eighteen hours earlier.

Nestled into a booth in the hotel lobby, Anessa proceeded to devour two bowls of Froot Loops with a large side of strawbabies. A tentative smile peeked out from behind her spoon with each bite.

As we shared the news of Anessa with close family and friends, the congratulatory and supportive messages flooded in. Everyone seemed genuinely happy for us, but I also imagined they were relieved to not feel as shitty about all the bad stuff we'd endured. The most common refrain I heard was how lucky Anessa was to have found us.

Lucky.

This time, instead of anger bubbling up at the word, I felt a chill as I was pulled back into the anxiety-inducing confines of the Child Protective Services conference room. I knew what people meant when they said this. Anessa's life would now be more stable, financially and emotionally. She would be showered with love and have everything else she needed. But isn't that what every child deserves? Anessa shouldn't be considered lucky for receiving consistent attention, nourishment, and care.

Is luck still considered luck if it is born out of trauma? Was Anessa lucky to have been pulled from her birth family before being placed in our car, greeted with a Minnie Mouse stuffie, and whisked off to an all-you-can-eat breakfast buffet? From the look on her face during those first few days with us, I can say with certainty that luck was not on her mind.

It has taken much unexpected heartache, disappointment, and reflection for me to accept what little control I have over my own life, let alone anyone else's. I can't predict what Anessa's emotional future will hold or how her early childhood trauma will affect her—and I hate that. I want to pretend that I can love her pain away, but I know first-hand that's not how healing works. I can, however, hold space for the life she had before she met us and answer her questions honestly. I can help her maintain relationships with her birth siblings and develop the emotional tools she will require as her understanding of her personal history grows. And oh my gosh, I can love her. But only time will tell how lucky Anessa feels, and her opinion is the only one that matters.

My rational brain yearns for direct cause-and-effect relationships and probably always will. I want to find the patterns, see the signs, and then learn from them so I can make better choices in the future. But try as I might, life has made it abundantly clear that not every balance sheet can be reconciled. Some events are a result of another, the next domino to fall, and some just happen. Are those events lucky? Has luck been the formidable adversary to my innate desire for control this whole time?

In "The Luckiest," Ben Folds sings about how lucky he is to have found his love, that all "the stumbles and falls" improbably brought them together. When Miguel and I danced to this song at our wedding, his words felt like they had been written for us. How lucky we were to have found each other amongst the millions of people in New York City, amongst the billions of people in the world.

But could Miguel and I still be lucky in love if the very product of that love, something as out of our control as genetics, brought us so much pain? Could Anessa still be lucky for finding her way into our family as the result of losing her first family? I'm not sure I will ever be able to answer these questions—but it is comforting to know that I am not alone in asking them. In fact, humankind has been pondering them for millennia, perhaps most famously in the Chinese parable of the farmer and the horse.

The story starts with a farmer who has saved and saved until he could afford to buy a new horse. Not long after the farmer purchases it and brings it home, the horse runs away. "So sorry for this bad news," his neighbor tells him. "Good news or bad news, can't say," the farmer replies. The next day, the horse returns and brings a stray horse with it. "What great news!" the farmer's son says. "Good news or bad news, can't say," the farmer replies.

A week passes, and the farmer's son is injured while riding the second horse. "What horrible news," the farmer's wife says. "Good news or bad news, can't say," the farmer replies. A month later, the king announces a war and orders that all able-bodied men be drafted into the army. "You are so lucky that your son was injured and cannot go," the farmer's neighbor tells him. "Good news or bad news, can't say," the farmer replies. And so the story goes.

As the parable illustrates, our perception of luck is influenced by the snapshot of time we are considering. Because it depends on the width of the frame through which it is viewed, luck is neither inherently good nor bad. Luck, like love, loss, and beauty, exists in the eye of the beholder, and by its very nature is as unpredictable as life itself.

AFTER BEARING WITNESS to the unpredictability of life, I had found some comfort in mitigating unknowns by moving our family back to the same New Jersey town we had lived in before Chicago. However, while the familiar faces and surroundings had allowed for a smoother transition, they were also reminders of a former me: a naive young mom not yet broken by the trauma and loss that awaited her. It was like going back in time and seeing a ghost of myself, but no matter how loudly I screamed, she couldn't hear my warnings.

Not long after bringing Anessa home, I took her to the pediatrician for a checkup. The nurse led us to one of the same exam rooms in which I had held Adelaide years before. After taking Anessa's height and weight, the nurse handed me a two-year milestone checklist. The veil between now and then felt so thin I could have closed my eyes and been back there again, holding Adelaide and that list of two-month milestones she would never fully achieve.

But I wasn't with Adelaide. I was with Anessa. And I didn't need to lean on denial to know that even if there were a few milestones on the list that Anessa couldn't do yet, with proper care and attention, she would. Here was the life I had envisioned with Adelaide, except I was going to experience it with Anessa.

Some might say this was part of God's plan, that everything happens for a reason. Many people told us there were larger forces at play when our family moved to Chicago, a city with excellent and accessible health care, just as our daughter was diagnosed with a complex medical condition. And it was certainly fortunate—though if some deity had decided to provide for our family with a financially secure job and move to a city better suited to our family's needs, you would think that same deity could have saved themselves a lot of work if they had just made Adelaide healthy in the first place.

Similarly, what kind of deity could justify sacrificing one daughter so that I might have another? There was no reason good enough, grand enough, beneficial enough, that it could justify Adelaide's death and our collective trauma and loss. Instead, I decided these unexplained events, the ones without a domino to point to, didn't have to have a reason, divine or otherwise. There is what we can control and what we can't. There are reasons and there is luck. If things don't happen for a reason, we can still make reason out of the things that happen. Some might say this is my way of regaining control over the uncontrollable. And they would probably be right. But that doesn't make me wrong.

Adelaide, and in turn Anessa, forced me to acknowledge there was only so much in life that was up to me. What I could control was the purpose I created out of the events I experienced, and that has brought me peace. Nothing can make the pain totally worth it, but that's not the point. I may never feel as lucky as I did dancing with my freshly minted husband, but there is no doubt that I have more gratitude now. Not gratitude that my daughter died, but that I got to know her. Not gratitude that Anessa faced the early childhood challenges she did, but that we get to love her and help her grow. Not gratitude that luck as a concept exists, but that it continues to inspire beautiful pieces of music and art.

It was slightly past bedtime one evening, roughly five months since Anessa had joined our family, and as I switched off the lights in her room, I heard her voice from behind. "Don't go!" she implored from her bed.

To help her feel safe in those first few months she was with us, I focused on maintaining a routine, and I had already read her stories, sang her songs, and tucked her in. I was nervous about setting a precedent of laying with her until she fell asleep—however, I had done exactly that countless times with both Jackson and Adelaide. Why didn't Anessa deserve the same comfort?

I returned to her bed, crawled in, and fell asleep right alongside her. All the lights had been turned off in the house by the time I made my way to my own bed. When Miguel felt me beside him, he rolled over, kissed me, and said, "I love seeing you so happy."

And I realized I was.

CHAPTER TWENTY-TWO
The Grower

In the first three years of Adelaide's life, I had been just as determined to discover what her overarching diagnosis was as I had been to help her get better. In part because I hoped if we knew the cause we would have a treatment—or at least some sort of direction in which to focus our efforts. But a diagnosis was also so much more. It would grant us entrance to a disease-specific community and provide a road map via a prognosis, as well as let us know any risk to future biological children.

Science didn't catch up to Adelaide during her life, but I remained committed to finding her diagnosis. In the weeks leading up to her death, I had worked with the Undiagnosed Diseases Network and Dr. Marcuccilli to coordinate the donation of Adelaide's brain. Perhaps someday, somewhere, a researcher would stumble across an answer.

Then, three and a half years later, in the spring of 2023, someone did.

A laboratory at McGill University in Canada was studying a gene called DENND5A, of which Adelaide had a variant. Both Miguel and Jackson carried the same variant and weren't affected, so initially we had ruled that out as a cause. But then the researchers discovered a mutation, hidden deep within my own DENND5A gene, that I had passed along to Adelaide but not Jackson. The researchers believed that this mutation had prevented Adelaide's neurons from forming correctly in utero.

On a Zoom call, our genetic counselor from the UDN explained that this was still a tentative diagnosis. Only thirty patients had been included in the study—the only known patients with this mutation in the world. No two patients had the same variant, and the sample size was too small to confirm with certainty, but everyone involved seemed confident that this likely contributed to Adelaide's various symptoms, particularly her drug-resistant epilepsy.

Meaning that from the moment Adelaide was a cluster of cells, this was always going to be her journey.

There is no cure for this broken gene, nothing even experimental. In fact, because this gene controls the initial development of stem cells in the brain, any treatment—had there been one—would have needed to be delivered in utero to be effective. To Miguel, this came as a relief, and I understood where he was coming from. How awful would it have been to discover that there was something else we could have done, or that some treatment could have become available only months or a year after we let her go? Now we knew for certain that we had done everything we could for her.

One might think I also would have welcomed this revelation. But releasing the fantasy of what could have been is complicated, especially when it undermines past decisions and sacrifices. The cross-country flights to get another opinion, the hours spent driving to different therapies, the time spent away from Jackson—it had all been in vain.

Darker yet, had we been hurting her by doing too much? How many futile procedures did we put her through? How much pain did I sign off on in the ignorant hope that this treatment, this therapy, this test would make a difference?

"I need a hug," I told Miguel when the call had ended. Locked in the safety of his arms, my tears stained his shirt. Good lord, was I grateful for the growth we had made, for how far we had come from the days of me crying alone on the bathroom floor and Miguel poking his head in to ask if I was okay. "I know this is a relief to you," I whispered, "but I'm not there yet."

"That's okay. It's a lot."

Rationally, I knew we had made the best decisions with the information available to us at the time. But I also knew I was going to need time to accept Adelaide's life for what it was always meant to be. Adelaide was not made to celebrate her next birthday, attend school, or play T-ball, because that wasn't her story. Years before, I had accepted that Adelaide's verbal, cognitive, and physical disabilities were as much a part of her as her dark blonde hair. However, accepting that her life was always going to be cut short, and there was never anything I could do about it, was another challenge altogether. There is a stark difference between acknowledging a truth and accepting its consequences.

WHILE DOING RESEARCH for my book, *Normal Broken*, I came across the work of a fascinating man named Stephen Jenkinson. Jenkinson has master's degrees in theology and social work from Harvard Divinity School and the University of Toronto, respectively, and used to work in palliative care, or what he calls the "death trade." Now in his early seventies, he was traveling the world performing a spoken word concert with multi-instrumental Gregory Hoskins called "Nights of Grief & Mystery." Naturally, when I saw he was coming to New York City, I bought tickets . . . and then promptly forgot that I had done so until days before the show.

Thank goodness for my cousin Maryclaire, who happened to not only be free but also game for this unusual event.

Should I invest in Kleenex? she texted me.

I don't think so, I texted back, but I packed a travel pack of tissues just in case.

That evening, as we took our seats at the Symphony Space theater on 95th and Broadway, I admitted to her that I had no idea what to expect from the evening.

"We shall adventure together," she responded with a smile.

A few minutes later, Stephen and Gregory walked onto a stage that had been sparsely set with a stool, chair, several microphones, a music stand, and a number of instruments, including a guitar, trumpet, small keyboard, and one of those foot pedal–operated audio looping machines.

The evening began with a beautiful song written from the point of view of a dying person who wishes their loved one could come with them—but, of course, they can't. I was immediately grateful that I had packed tissues, though not nearly as grateful as I was when, twenty minutes into the performance, Stephen pivoted to talking about the death of children. I was not prepared. Typically, even people who talk about death and grief steer clear of childhood death, as it is deemed taboo and too uncomfortable. Maryclaire took my hand and didn't let go.

Stephen clearly wasn't a typical person, though, and he confronted head-on our culture's general belief that children aren't supposed to die. That they shouldn't die; that it's cruel and unfair. The problem is that sometimes they do. This thing that is not supposed to happen happens—and then what?

Unfortunately, Stephen noted, age is not factored into the circle of life, and there is no should, supposed to, or fairness about it. To assume otherwise does not serve the dying or their families. Then Stephen shared the story of a little girl he'd met who was dying from leukemia. Her family was understandably distraught about the loss of both their child and the full life they felt she was being cheated out of.

I squeezed Maryclaire's hand and tried to swallow the sob closing in on my throat. *What in the actual hell was I thinking, buying tickets to this show?* But I was in it now. I couldn't get up and I didn't want to.

As Stephen's story progressed, far more poetic and melodic than my retelling here, he spoke directly to the dying girl, telling her that her family was upset because she wouldn't get to live a full life. To which the little girl scoffed, as only little girls can, and replied with a list of the amazing yet everyday experiences she'd had.

This, I realized, was the root of my resistance to Adelaide's diagnosis. I couldn't accept that a fuller life was never possible for her. Was that just my perception of her life, though?

If Adelaide could have spoken to me, if I had ever thought to ask her this question, how would she have responded?

That night, back in the comfort of my bed, I imagined what a similar conversation with Adelaide might look like.

Hey, baby girl. I miss you. So I saw this guy talking about living a full life, and I wondered if you feel like you got to live a full life.

Mommy, what are you talking about? What about when I got to ride horses in therapy or put my feet in the ocean? What about my morning cuddles with Jackson and my evening cuddles with you? What about dancing with Daddy? What about my afternoon walks with Nurse Alison when I felt the wind on my cheeks and heard the birds in the trees? What about all the people I got to meet who held my hand and spoke to me? What about how much my family loves me?

And she would be right. Because who determines what qualifies as a full life? The more I thought about it, the sillier it seemed to measure fullness by the number of days someone lived, the distances they traveled, or the achievements they earned. I'm not sure I know enough about enough to say for sure what would qualify—but my guess is it would have something to do with knowing and feeling love. And if that's the case, then my little ladybug lived a life as full as anyone could wish for.

I was surviving and healing, and I now understood that there would always be, if not new asteroids, at least the fragmented shards of past asteroids to work around. My hard-earned healing had become positive growth, but I wasn't prepared for that very growth to unexpectedly reignite my grief.

"Mommy! Mommy! Mommy! Can I have your phone?"

We hadn't even sat down on the baseball field bleachers, and Anessa was reaching for my purse like a fiend looking for their next hit. I used to feel bad that Anessa got dragged to all her brother's baseball games—until I realized that she was living her best barely supervised, snack-eating, phone-watching life.

I unlocked my phone to hand to Anessa, and a picture of Jackson and Adelaide cuddling on our couch in Chicago stared back at me, courtesy of the phone's "Memories" feature. They were both in their pj's with Jackson's arms around Adelaide in a possessive cuddle while watching TV. It was just a picture, but I could still hear Adelaide's grunts of protest as she tried to loosen herself from her brother's embrace. This image, which had been so mundane, so routine to me just half a decade ago, was now relegated to memories—apparently literally as well as digitally.

I stared at Adelaide's face for just a moment, trying to decipher the mixture of emotions I was feeling like a sommelier separating out flavor notes in a glass of wine. Usually, when I happened upon photos of Adelaide, I could easily label my feelings as some form of loss and love. But this time it was muddled—or maybe I was resisting. Before I could land on the right combination, I swiped away from the picture to the folder labeled "Anessa's Games." I handed the phone over to an impatient and fidgety Anessa, who immediately calmed when the weight of her dopamine fix hit her hands.

I let the usual on-field and off-field activities surrounding me suck me in. And I pushed aside the picture and its corresponding emotions—until that night, anyway, when it all came back unbidden just as my head was hitting the pillow.

I'd seen that exact photo dozens of times and with the flip of an internal switch could see it once again, as if projected on a screen in my mind. Again, I tried to assess my emotional response.

First had come shock. The shock of being thrust back into what had once been normal, but now felt foreign. The collision of two worlds, two lives, two different Kellys.

Guilt was quick to follow—because how could that photo shock me? That was *my* daughter, that was *our* life. How had I allowed so much distance to grow between my past and present selves?

Then grief settled in like a weighted blanket, at once heavy and comforting. I saw Adelaide's cheeks, her tousled hair, her belly with its G-tube visible under her hiked-up pj top. I imagined checking the numbers on her pulse oximeter, which wasn't in the picture but was always close by, to be sure Jackson wasn't hugging her too tightly.

Not to be outdone, guilt reclaimed its top position as I realized: missing Adelaide hadn't been my first reaction. And then I had done something even more egregious. I'd swiped the photo away, handed the phone to my new daughter, and returned my attention to the baseball game. I moved on, just as I'd imagined others had when they learned of her death in the news.

The familiar signs of anxiety revved up. My heart raced and swelled as if it might burst from my chest. I tried to re-center myself in the physical world of my bedroom. Behind me, Miguel had his bedside light on and was mindlessly scrolling through his own dopamine time suck. The light cast my shadow, lying in bed, on the wall.

I knew the shadow was mine, yet I felt detached from it, as if at any moment it could get up and walk away like Peter Pan's. But I wasn't a lost boy yearning to be a child forever.

Adelaide would always be almost four, eternally a child, frozen in time. Meanwhile, I was aging, growing, and living. My life moved forward while she stayed behind. Her memory no longer consumed my every waking moment, and the grief tied to it had lessened its hold on me. I'd known it would happen eventually. I just hadn't known when.

And then I finally realized what that photo had triggered in me: it was a new kind of grief. Not grief for having lost my daughter, but for the passage of time between Adelaide's frozen place and my fluid one. It was a grief thickly coated in guilt, because how could I let Adelaide's memory drift so far from my regular thoughts?

But even as I clocked the guilt, I knew this was the next natural step on my healing journey. Progress isn't pretty. It's gritty and often resented, but it can still be positive. Like a caterpillar devolving into goo before it transforms into a butterfly, I was growing into the next version of myself, and the process was as ill-fitting and uncomfortable as ever.

CHAPTER TWENTY-THREE
The Nesting Doll

Anessa had been with us for two years. She was now officially adopted, and most of the time, it felt like she had always been here—certainly in the way she and Jackson bickered. As annoying as their spats could be, however, they were tinged with nostalgia as I remembered pranks and fights with my own brother.

After spending his twenties teaching English in Costa Rica, Cam had attended law school before eventually settling back in Omaha. There he met Danielle, his wonderful wife, who I adore if for no other reason (though there are many) than the fact she calls him on his bullshit. I wouldn't put it past Cam to enter a room and demand that everyone refer to him as Batman in his thirties, just as he had when he was two.

Before their wedding the previous summer, Cam and Danielle had asked Anessa to be one of their flower girls. I had always dreamed of Adelaide being a flower girl in someone's wedding, ideally Cameron's, but as he liked to remind me, the timeline of his love life was not up to me. I'm not sure where my desire to have Adelaide be a flower girl came from. I think I felt it was a rite of little girl passage, like cutting your own bangs—except that it was something that Adelaide would have been capable of doing, had she lived long enough.

Now, though, I was excited to share this rite of passage with my second daughter.

Anessa was equally excited, though more so about the ivory and gold sparkly dress to which we added a small ladybug in memory of Adelaide. I convinced myself that, at least in spirit, both my girls had been part of the bridal party. I was healing; this was growth.

Jackson had been a junior groomsman and looked dashing in a light grey suit that matched the rest of the groomsmen. Currently, however, he was dressed in the typical preteen uniform of sweatpants and a hoodie, with the personal style addition of a beanie over long hair that he had grown out during the pandemic to match his dad's.

"Anessa! Get out of my room!" Jackson yelled. He was eleven and suddenly very concerned with his privacy, a concept that four-year-old Anessa was years from understanding or respecting.

Never one to back down from a fight, Anessa snatched something from Jackson's desk and stood just far enough away that Jackson would have to get up from his chair, thus pausing his video game, to reach her.

While I simultaneously appreciated how typical their relationship had become and debated whether I should intervene or let them work it out, the doorbell rang. Both dogs sprang to life, barking and herding me to the door. Awaiting me was our neighbor Ruby, now eight, holding my old Pound Puppy Jessica and her plastic house, bowl, and bone.

"We're cleaning out my room, and my mom said to see if you want this back because I don't play with it anymore," Ruby said, holding out Jessica inside her doghouse.

"Thank you, Ruby. I'm sure Anessa will love her," I said. With her mission accomplished, Ruby turned to go. "Tell your mom thank you!" I yelled as she headed back across the street.

Realizing there would be no new source of attention, the dogs returned to their previously disrupted naps. In their wake stood

Anessa on the stairs, lured from tormenting her brother by the fuss at the door.

"Was that Ruby? Does she want to play with me? What's that?" Anessa asked in rapid succession.

"This is a toy I gave to Ruby a couple of years ago. It used to be mine when I was little, and now it's yours," I said, handing the toy over to Anessa's outstretched arms.

"A present! For me? Thank you!" Anessa squealed. She took Jessica out of her house and examined her big plastic eyes before asking, "What's her name?"

"I called her Jessica, but you can name her whatever you want," I answered.

"It's okay, I think her name is still Jessica."

And so Jessica, the lone survivor of the trunk that I had lugged in denial back and forth across the country, came home to my daughter.

Between flower girl dresses and Pound Puppies, Anessa was allowing me to experience parenting a neurotypical daughter. With her, so many of the dreams I'd held for Adelaide were coming true. It was the very definition of bittersweet. I tried so hard to live in the moment with Anessa, while also giving the conflicting emotions of the past their own space and time. One experience didn't have to have anything to do with the other. They could be separate, just as my two daughters were their own individuals. I just wished they didn't have to exist each on their own timeline—that they could know each other.

Loss has led me to rethink time, how it unfolds, repeats, or builds. Like layers of a nesting doll, each new iteration of myself has taken its initial shape from the version that came before. I can feel the ways past events have contoured the present—but no matter how hard I try to reshape myself in imitation of the past, I have never been able recreate an exact copy.

Perhaps more importantly, I no longer wish to.

Still, as my life has unfolded so disparately from my expectations, naive or otherwise, I've struggled to understand: How do I remain true to myself? And what is it exactly that I am trying to stay true to? Especially when every layer—desired or not—is now a part of me. It hasn't escaped me that I use my acting lessons to enhance my stage presence when I deliver a keynote. That I draw from my event and sales experience when I assist on a fundraising campaign. Or that I harness my experiences as a mom, caregiver, and advocate in my writing.

Over time, I've realized that who I am has been an evolution—which means how I stay true to myself must evolve as well. Could it really be as simple as fulfilling my current life responsibilities while embracing what brings me joy, even while knowing that both my responsibilities and joy will change over time? If sense of self is fluid (not unlike grief), then it follows that pursuit of self would be in continuous flux as well. There will be no finish line, no moment of enlightenment, but instead, and hopefully, a life well lived.

The very coalescence of control and luck.

As I WRITE this, the four-year anniversary of Adelaide's passing draws closer. I have been dreading passing this threshold since she died: Adelaide will soon have been gone longer than she was alive. It's hard to make sense of this inconceivable passage of time. How is it possible? How could so much meaning, life, and love have been crammed into four years? What even is time?

I hate how helpless I am to stop the growing chasm between her life and the present, as well as the perspective it forces—one where Adelaide was merely a fraction of my life, an inch on my timeline. But that perspective could never account for the range of enduring impacts, from catastrophic to euphoric, she had on me. Time isn't justifying my emotions the way I need it to, or maybe I'm giving time too much power.

There is a noticeable threshold that children cross when they begin to understand the concept of time. Countless tantrums are avoided once they can count how many sleeps remain until an exciting event and can comprehend (and trust) that "later" doesn't mean "never." But like all cognitive development, this comes in stages. For Anessa, at four, anything happening in the future happens tomorrow. Anything in the past was last night. This means she had her birthday party (in February) last night and we are going trick-or-treating (in one month) tomorrow. There is something freeing in viewing time as simply the past, present, and future. Obviously, this presents challenges for navigating complicated family and work schedules. But maybe Anessa is onto something, at least when it comes to memories and their places in time.

Several Christmases ago, I gave Mom and Dad a digital picture frame that now sits on a shelf in their living room. During a recent summer visit, Anessa was absolutely mesmerized by it. The photos rotated randomly, each new photo pausing for several seconds before transitioning to the next, as if turning the page in a very disorganized family photo album. Perched on the edge of an overstuffed chair, Anessa loudly announced to anyone in earshot whose picture was now being displayed, adding extra enthusiasm when it was a picture of herself.

"Mommy! It's you and Daddy! You look fancy . . . Aw, it's baby Adelaide! She's so cute . . . Mommy! Come look! It's me! It's me!"

Everything contained in those thousands of pixels happened, as Anessa would say, "last night." In that frame, time and the memories made within are tangled together like limbs cuddling under a blanket. In that frame, Adelaide and Anessa were intertwined, coexisting in a shared past tense. It was a place where a memory's distance from the present had no bearing on its importance.

Adelaide may only have shared life with us for three years and 360 days, but those years and days were some of the fullest and most vibrant of my life. Thankfully, my life continues, and I hope there are many more full and vibrant days to come, but these new days won't diminish the value or importance of my love for Adelaide and the time we spent together. Especially when it was only last night that Adelaide squeezed my finger for the last time, and Anessa asked to hold my hand for the first time, and Jackson asked me to tuck him in, and Miguel asked me to marry him.

In a tangled last night, we are all together.

And in an undefined tomorrow, we all will be again.

I WAS CLEARING out a cabinet in our hallway credenza, which had become a dumping ground for all the things that didn't have a place. Candles, tablecloths, platters, and holiday decorations littered the floor.

"Oooh, what's this?" Anessa asked, holding up a narrow green box.

"It's a wind chime," I said, opening the box and showing her the beautiful arrangement of brass and wood.

Anessa, ever curious, needed to know more, specifically what it did and what the words etched on the wood pendulum said.

"In memory of Adelaide Grace," I read aloud. "It was given to us so that every time we hear the chimes ring, we can be reminded of Adelaide. Tell you what, why don't you help me hang it up on the back patio?"

Days later, we were coming home after school when a slight breeze stirred the chimes on an otherwise windless day. Just a minute earlier or later, and we would have missed it. I smiled to myself as the twinkles faded, idly wondering whether this was luck or design at play.

"Hello, Adelaide!" Anessa said, skipping toward the door. Then she stopped short and turned to look back at me as if she was waiting for something. "Mommy, you need to say hi. Adelaide is ringing for us."

My breath caught. "Hi, baby girl," I whispered.

Here, in this life, in defiance of time and in deference to luck, my daughters were talking to each other—a part of each other's stories and forever living through mine.

ACKNOWLEDGMENTS

If there is one aspect of my life where I truly feel the luckiest, it is that I have such wonderful people surrounding me. In this fourth iteration of my career there is no one I am luckier to have on my professional team than my agent, the unflappable Courtney Paganelli, with LGR Literary Agency. Thank you for believing in me and this book, for reading countless drafts, and for holding my hand (again) every step of the way.

Thank you to BenBella publishing for their collaborative effort, specifically editors Victoria Carmody and Leah Wilson, copyeditor Leah Baxter, cover artists Morgan Carr and Sarah Avinger, and marketing director Lindsay Marshall. It was incredible to work with an all-woman team, many of whom are mothers.

This book would suck if not for all the people who read early drafts or assisted on certain chapters: my writing coach extraordinaire Marcelle Soviero, my crazy talented writing group TBWP, especially Patty Hamrick, Andrew Laing, Peter Kazon, Vanessa Walters, Helen Epstein, and Olga Jobe. And also dear friends: Mel Green, Bud Hager, Dr. Wendy Borlabi, Jasmine Swann, and Vadim Feichner.

As I said in the book, I do not believe that things happen for a reason, but that we can make reason out of the things that happen. Thank you to the following organizations for helping me find the reason:

The CURE Epilepsy team past and present gave me purpose when I was lost. Science couldn't catch up to Adelaide, but I will not stop fighting by your side to help science push forward for the next patient and their family.

Everyone at the Undiagnosed Diseases Network and the UDN Foundation. Thank you for never giving up on finding a diagnosis and for giving hope to the zebras among the horses. A special thank you to the scientists at McGill University, especially Dr. Peter McPherson and Dr. Emily Banks, who gave us answers and eventually peace.

A massive thank you to the team at Nix Patterson Law and my fellow defendants who helped prosecute James Toback under New York's Adult Survivors Act, ultimately leading to a guilty verdict. Meeting other victims and testifying in court brought me the closure I had sought for decades. Hopefully other young women will learn that this shame is not yours, and that experiences like mine are indeed criminal.

Thank you to the people who taught me the lessons I needed most: Mr. Terry Peterson for nurturing my ambition and supporting me for nearly thirty years. Susan Axelrod for guiding me through the epilepsy community and spearheading life-changing research. Lauren Schrero for teaching me the power of empathy and the underestimated strength of disability. Dr. Marcuccilli for showing me not just what healthcare should look like, but what it should feel like. Ady and my Hayden's House mamas for creating a space where I could be normal broken. Lori Rabb for an email and a best friend I couldn't live without.

Every few years I collect a new lifelong friend who has no idea what they are getting into with me, but for some reason sticks around. Brittany, nothing makes me happier than seeing you live out your wanderlust dreams. I only wish it didn't have to take you so far away. Courtney, I do not know what I would do without you. Kristin and Lindsay, your friendship proves that laughter is the best medicine. Jeff, you were right. Jenilyn, you truly are a fairy of light and love. Erin, I always wanted a big sister, thank you for being mine. Bakari, asante kwa kunifundisha.

Marc, I save you, you save me. Stacy, you are the very embodiment of friendship. Maryclaire, the best hand-holder there has ever been. Anne, how lost I would have been in Chicago without you. Jenny, you are my soul sister. Lindsay, like two sides of an arch we will keep each other standing. There are so many more from NJ to LA and everywhere in between that have held me and our family up throughout the years. I love you all.

If trauma can be inherited, then I believe the same can be said for strength. For that I am grateful to my relatives that came before me, particularly my grandmothers and great-grandmothers. Mom, this book would not exist without you—and not just for the obvious reasons—but because you have always believed I could do wonderful things and then supported me and my family to be sure that I did. Dad, thank you for instilling in me a robust voice of reason, a great sense of humor, and an even greater taste in music. So many other family members have stepped up when I needed them most including Mary, Cam, Danielle, Wendy, and my Chicago cousin crew. You all mean the world to me.

Thank you to my beautiful children for inspiring every word of this book. I view my entire life through the lens of being your mother. Each of you has made my life richer in wildly different ways, all while teaching me grace with a patience that is far beyond your years.

And to the man that makes me the luckiest of all, my Mig. Maybe someday our life will be a little less exciting, and we'll be able to sit back and marvel at all we've survived, created, and inspired. In the meantime, as long as you're by my side, these rockets and parachutes don't stand a chance. I love you more than you love hot sauce.

ABOUT THE AUTHOR

KELLY CERVANTES is an award-winning writer, speaker, and epilepsy, rare disease, and grief advocate. Her debut book, *Normal Broken*, was a USA Today bestseller. She has been published in the *Chicago Tribune*, *Cosmopolitan*, and *Fortune* as well as featured on *MSNBC*, *NY Times*, and *CNN*. She sits on the boards of CURE Epilepsy and The Undiagnosed Diseases Network Foundation and hosts CURE Epilepsy's podcast, *Seizing Life*. Born and raised in the Midwest, Kelly resides in Maplewood, New Jersey, with her family.